W9-CHT-354

Warm Regards,

Maxine Sterling

Days of
Stein and Roses

Days of
Stein and Roses

Martie Sterling

DODD, MEAD & COMPANY
NEW YORK

Some parts of this book have appeared in Ski Magazine in a different version.

Copyright © 1984 by Martie Sterling
All rights reserved
No part of this book may be reproduced in any form without permission in writing from the publisher.
Published by Dodd, Mead & Company, Inc.
79 Madison Avenue, New York, N.Y. 10016
Distributed in Canada by
McClelland and Stewart Limited, Toronto
Manufactured in the United States of America
Designed by Roxana Laughlin
First Edition

Library of Congress Cataloging in Publication Data

Sterling, Martie.
  Days of Stein and roses.

  1. Heatherbed Lodge (Aspen, Colo.)   2. Aspen (Colo.)—
Hotels, motels, etc.   3. Hotel management—Colorado—
Aspen.   4. Ski resorts—Colorado—Aspen.   I. Title.
TX941.H43S74   1984   647'.94788'4301   84–8194
ISBN 0–396–08480–X

*This book is my loving
legacy to my family.*

Contents

Acknowledgments

I wish to thank my devoted reader Roddy Burdine; the ladies of the Pitkin County Library who are always available to research the Aspen silver output of 1893 and the ephemeral usages of *which* and *that*; and my friend Mort Lund — I am terrible at titles, and he gave me this one.

In many cases, names have been changed to protect the innocent and the guilty.

Days of
Stein and Roses

∗ Book I

GETTING
THERE

Getting Out of Pennsylvania

WHOEVER SAID that quiz programs are a sop to the heaving masses was not looking at things from the contestant's point of view. Take the father of nine who leapt from grease pit to graduate school after cleaning up on "Name That Tune." The woman who spent years waiting on tables and an alcoholic father, then won on "Hollywood Squares," institutionalized the old man and has been happily digging potsherds in the Negev ever since. Or the beautician who fled straight from "Family Feud" to Rio, where he is blissfully cutting amethysts instead of hair.

And then of course there's me.

I was a contestant on "Tic Tac Dough" and went from the Junior League to junior ski racing in ten easy wins.

It was a cinch for my husband, Ken, to pull up stakes and head for snow country—his mother had been frightened by a musk-ox while carrying him. As for me, I was suckered by an Andrè of Montreal ski creation with padded Joan Crawford shoulders. But I can tell you that our children were pretty bewildered. Back in the late fifties it wasn't easy giving up an effete country club life in the East for an Aspen, Colorado ski lodge, a future devoid of television, an upside-down septic tank, a house teeming with Norwegian aliens, a folk hero named Stein, one

Rocky Mountain hunkered down in your lap, and another looming at your rear.

Even I might have been deterred had I known how wild the West, how high the mountains, how deep the snow. And if Ken had suspected how many hundreds of people we'd be having for dinner and to spend the night, I believe he might have sought refuge in the nearest Trappist monastery.

All of this was not as abrupt as it sounds, as I'd been trying to get out of Pennsylvania since I was five. Even as a child I sensed there was more to life than the Delaware & Lackawanna Railroad, coal towns with permanent ring-around-the-collar, interminable sunless winters, and rows of brick houses clustered together like people sharing an umbrella.

I remember banker's gray March days, pewter gray December days, and grizzled skies that dripped and poured sleet, rain, drizzle, and snow. My girlhood winters teemed with six-buckle galoshes and woolen snowsuits, and scarves and mittens so soon sopping wet and leaden that I staggered in from the coasting hill thoroughly drenched, weighing a ton, bawling with pain and hating winter.

I know now that my childhood sometimes seemed dreary because it was spent in the Great Depression. It's no wonder people and places looked like tattletale gray wash hung out on a line. Following Black Thursday (plus Gloomy Tuesday, Suicide Friday, and other hallmark dates too numerous to mention), Mother and Daddy, like plenty of young couples, had their mettles sorely tested. The grim spectres of bread and soup lines, bankruptcy courts, closed caskets, Hooverville shantytowns, and beady-eyed bill collectors were everywhere.

This was especially hard on Mother. She had perfect pitch and had been practicing on her Steinway six hours a day for years. She had acquired a collection of full-length lace concert gowns cut on the bias and was all set to make her Carnegie Hall debut. Like an Olympic runner poised at the starting line when the gun won't go off, she was forced to straighten up and reset her sights—from armloads of long-stemmed roses and sheaves of glowing reviews to piles of ledgers and stacks of smelly, unsightly tires.

At Daddy's baccalaureate services, he had met and shaken the hand of Mr. Harvey Firestone and found himself up to his eyeballs in the rubber business. We children used to pray he'd meet and shake the hand of Miss Fanny Farmer or Mr. F. A. O. Schwartz and become immersed in some worthy enterprise where we could sample the merchandise. He did have an opportunity to invest in a newfangled machine that sliced potatoes and toasted them in thin salty chips, but he said to Mother, "I don't believe it will go." Pretty soon it didn't matter what business he was in, as no one was making a killing anyhow.

Mother was made of stern stuff and she didn't whine. She switched from Beethoven sonatas to double-digit bookkeeping without even shifting gears. And although our Christmases grew sparse and the meatloaf full of bread crumbs, and our shoes quarter, half, then fully resoled, we made it through the Depression.

After Roosevelt was elected, he took the country by the scruff of the neck and shook it until gradually it began to straighten out. The tramps we fed on our back porch came less often. Shantytowns melted away. Men found work with the C.C.C. and the W.P.A. and were able to go off hated "relief." And I finally stopped dreaming about the poorhouse, where our hired girls warned us children that ill-behaved inmates were fed watery cabbage soup and toenail pairings.

During these years I went through phases, like the moon. In the cold ache of winter I hibernated, except for brief sorties to school, the library, or the coasting hill. With the coming of spring, I'd hear the call of the wild and begin toughening up my shooting thumb with lemon rind and salt and tracking down my skate key.

At seventeen I graduated from high school with a suppurating case of poison ivy drooling down my legs and a lump bobbing around my throat. Pearl Harbor was six months old, all the boys were going off to war, and my best friend Gracie and I just knew we'd end our days as shriveled old maids. I was so bemused I forgot four typewritten pages of my valedictory address, a lapse which noticeably improved the speech. I went south to college with three bathing suits, two trunks, my golf clubs, and a burning desire to stay warm. If I did marry, I decided, it might as well be some nice, mush-mouthed boy who would settle me in a hot and humid climate.

Duke University lies in the fetid flats of Durham, North Carolina, where the tobacco fumes are so thick you become a nicotine addict whether you smoke or not. With the war raging on all fronts, five thousand all-American boys catapulted through Duke's Navy V-12 program with such speed that just as you puckered up for your first good night kiss, the guy was whisked out to sea. The atmosphere was frenzied, and for a couple of years I felt very unsettled.

I knitted ugly, khaki-colored balaclavas and mufflers in the dark of movie theaters, making so many mistakes that they were laced with lumps and gaps; stood in block-long lines for cigarettes and silk stockings and, when there weren't any cigarettes, rolled my own from local dregs; plastered my legs with pancake makeup; during vacations drove for the American Women's Volunteer Service at the local Navy depot; operated a fork lift and administered driving tests to hundreds of ensigns with terminal dyslexia.

We girls on the Duke swim team not only endured an austerity era of no blow dryers, curling irons, or hot rollers, but as the war accelerated also gave up competing in the butterfly and backstroke and devoted our efforts to teaching future Navy officers how to tread water.

Finally, after slipping out a dorm window to meet a late

date and dropping into the arms of a delighted campus cop, I was encouraged to transfer to another school.

Thus began my unwitting odyssey to ski and frostbite country.

Syracuse University is in the New York State snow belt where the weather freezes you right to your pancreas. Despite the cold, the school was so stimulating it brought even my gelid blood to a rolling boil.

Insulated in a Hudson's Bay blanket coat, knee-length pink snuggies, and fleece-lined stadium boots, I slithered from class to class like a mackerel on a block of ice. My nose ran and my eyes watered but I scarcely noticed. I was in hog heaven studying drama, advertising, creative writing, oil painting, interior design, and medieval history. By the time I graduated, I felt fully prepared to edit a newspaper, slipcover a chair, promote a perfume, write an opera, manage a radio station and inhabit the ateliers of New York and Rome.

The only thing I was not prepared for was Iglook, Son of the Far North. Since those early Depression days of sodden snowsuits, not only ice and snow but also bald trees, frozen desserts, and Sonja Henie movies had left me cold. I'd headed south to Duke to escape the wintry blasts of Pennsylvania, for heaven's sake. The last thing I had in mind was to run afoul of and fall for a man who was a spiritual descendant of Nanook of the North.

Kenneth Robinson Sterling was weaned on New Hampshire winters and reared with Russians, Poles, Finns, and moose. He grew up in a town where madmen of all ages started praying for snow in September so the skiing and the ice hockey could start a little early that year. At Syracuse he spent large unwholesome amounts of time out-of-doors in howling gales campaigning for student office, singing under sorority house windows, plowing through hip-deep snow to the library and blithely courting pneumonia.

I didn't know any of this the day a big, breezy man sat

two seats from me in a poli sci. lecture knitting an argyle sock. I too was knitting an argyle sock and had just rounded the bend of the heel with the same finesse I'd employed on all those khaki mufflers. Suddenly a large, hairy hand reached down the row, took my sock, unraveled the heel and reknitted it swiftly—and right. This singular behavior attracted a lot of unwelcome attention, especially mine and the professor's.

Later I learned that the weirdo had already had pneumonia, followed by TB, both brought on by rowing on the Syracuse crew in the icy storms of Lake Onondaga. In high school he had been "All New England Football," "Most Conceited," "Best Dressed," and a great big bore. After tearing apart two hospitals and several sanatoriums, he finally resigned himself to awaiting the discovery of antibiotics, appreciating opera and knitting a mean pair of baby booties.

I thought he was adorable and spent long hours in the Big Orange listening giddily as he and his fraternity brothers drank beer and extolled heavy winter snowfalls. Mostly they raved over an esoteric sport called "skiing." Their descriptions ranged from "bombing the mountain" to "taking a dive," "flaming out," and "crashing and burning"—all of which gave me an uneasy feeling that the war was still on and that this skiing was for kamikaze personalities. That's what I felt, right up to the moment I euphorically permitted myself to become pinned. Then engaged. And finally married.

Naturally the wedding was Mother's idea. But I didn't want to be peevish about it. Everyone was sick of the sacrifices of war, and who was I to deprive a woman of the best excuse she ever had for a monumental drunk? There was a sit-down dinner for three hundred, carloads of fresh poinsettias, and an orchestra for dancing, and Mother was happy.

The honeymoon? That was Iglook's idea.

CHAPTER 2

The Chair Was
Not Electric

As we rolled through the Canadian north, the groom snoring softly on the wicker seat beside me, I stared dismally out on a landscape as black as my mood and wondered for the fiftieth time, "What am I doing here?"

I knew good and well what I was doing there. I was headed for a resort that sounded unpleasantly like some sort of winter ague, to a place called Mont Tremblant in the Laurentian Mountains and the Province de Quebec. It was north of the 50th Parallel and the permafrost line. I was, for God's sake, going skiing.

Listen, nowadays millions of people ski. Ski shops, ski resorts, ski magazines, movies, and books abound. Back then it was a different story. The only suckers who skied were Ken's cronies, a few Austrian and Scandinavian refugees, the boys in the Dartmouth Outing Club, and a handful of misguided eastern millionaires.

Ken had been at it since before Lindbergh soloed the Atlantic; before Bunny Bertram built the first rope tow at Suicide Six; before Tony Matt schussed the Headwall. Ski-wise, this put him in a class with pre-Columbian art.

"Why?" I'd implored with tears in my eyes. "Why can't we go to a warm Caribbean beach like all the other honeymooners we know? Canada?" I'd wailed. "In January?"

"Listen, honey, once you try skiing I promise you'll be hooked for life."

"To say nothing of frozen solid," I muttered rudely.

Warming myself in the glow of my engagement ring, I'd tried to think of skiing as a passing phase, like thumb sucking. That's what I'd tried to think, right up to the fix I now found myself in, shaken with cold and self-doubt and headed straight for the arctic tundra.

The train Iglook and I were riding had been resurrected from the Victoria & Albert Museum for war duty, and our honeymoon had begun in the inauspicious manner of immigrants fleeing the Old Country via steerage. Gusts of snow whipped through cracks in the worn floorboards and eddied around my frozen feet. A puny potbellied stove at the far end of the car had given up the ghost and now served as seating space for extra passengers. The car was jammed to the platforms with Canadian woodsmen returning flat broke and stinking drunk from Christmas holiday in Montreal.

None of them spoke English and neither, it developed, did *le conducteur*. It was an added blow for me to find, after ten years of French literature and membership in the French honorary fraternity, Phi Kappa Phooey, that I was unable to make myself understood, while Iglook, on the casual basis of lifelong friendships with a number of French Canucks, conversed easily with everyone.

"Bastard French, honey," he explained chattily.

French Canadians on their own turf are called *habitants*, and soon *les habitants* were singing French carols and folk songs, accompanying themselves with flamenco-like heel and toe tapping, their palms slapping knees and thighs in a beat so catchy I began to warm to the merriment.

The trouble was that we stayed too late at the ball. By the time we made dozens of station stops, halted at intervals for animals, both wild and domestic, on the tracks, stopped to shovel snowdrifts and paused to greet train-men's kinfolk along the route, the tone and tenor of the party had deteriorated badly.

"They're all drunker than boiled owls," I whispered to Ken through clenched teeth.

"Well, I just wish they'd pass one of those jugs back this way," he said.

"For Lord's sake, why?"

"Because it's cold in here, and you refuse to neck."

This terrified me. If Ken confessed to being chilled, hypothermia could not be far behind.

"Listen," I hissed, "it's bad enough that we're dressed for a reception with the queen. One little love scene, and we could easily trigger a riot." Pulling my opossum coat over my chin like a Muslim veil, I inched unobtrusively closer to my groom.

We lovers sat rigidly side by side as more miles, hours, and station stops rattled by, and the singing degenerated into what Ken said was the dirty French version of "Little Red Wing." Even the Son of the Far North was growing edgy. "Talk about life in the raw," he muttered as two *voyageurs* unsheathed vicious hunting knives and began snarling and slashing at each other.

There were also camp followers. At least I was pretty sure they were camp followers when a couple of them began brawling over one of the men in the most ear-splitting cat fight I'd seen this side of Cecil B. DeMille. I believe that Ken, along with me, now felt our chances of climbing off that train unscathed had dimmed to fifty-fifty.

"Saint Adele! . . . Val David!" roared *le conducteur* above the clamor. "Saint Agathe! . . . Saint Jovite!" It was impossible to tell if he was calling on all the saints for succor or merely announcing station stops. At last, in a voice so lost in the drunken din that we nearly missed it, he croaked, "Tremblant Station."

A small, dark, ferret-faced man in a tasseled cap embraced Ken under the mistaken impression that he was

"Pierre, *mon ami!*" By the time we'd shaken him off we were barely able to hurl bags, skis, trunks, and poles onto the platform and leap after them as the train lurched drunkenly off into the night. It had taken us eight and one-half hours to travel less than ninety miles.

The Tremblant Station was very little improvement over the Tremblant train. It was roughly the size of a four-man ice-fishing shack, and its Tooterville Trolley interior was not your showcase urban waiting room. The furnishings consisted of one ten-watt light bulb dangling at the end of a frayed cord, an ancient coal stove feebly reaching out with a ray or two of heat, a varnished oak bench, a Bull Durham thermometer that had struck bottom and burst, and a loudly ticking wall clock that announced the time as 1:25 A.M. The year 1947 had arrived, and we'd missed its entrance entirely.

Since we were seven hours late, we were not exactly expecting a ticker tape reception. Instead we held hands and hunched down in our coats with the air of an expeditionary party not anticipating reinforcements any time soon. Just as I was visualizing our stiff bodies frozen in tragic tableau, a shrill "Ka-dooooooooooo-kah!" shredded the silence. "Allo in zair," yelled Kadookah, and we were saved.

Our rescuer was a disgruntled habitant who had the consummate good sense to disapprove of skiers and show it. He drove us to the Inn answering our many babbling questions in stony monosyllables. It wasn't his fault that the train was a day late, and he'd wasted a perfectly good New Year's Eve venturing into the subzero night after a couple of damn fool newlyweds.

Thus I learned my first lesson in ski resorts. They are frequently hell to get to. This makes sense. As Ken has pointed out over the years, we can't expect to find five-thousand-foot mountains and millions of cubic feet of snow within easy reach of a short cab fare, now can we? Lesson number two was that ski lodges, whether modest or imposing, have a giddy splendor all their own. The thing is, they're there when you need them most—following avalanche, blizzard, vehicular pileup, or near death from freezing.

By no stretch of semantics could the Inn at Mont Tremblant have been termed modest. To me it was an amalgam of the Pitti Palace and Windsor Castle. A twelve-log fire chuckled and chattered from the most enormous fireplace I'd ever seen. Garlands of pine boughs and a Bunyonesque Christmas tree scented the air with an incense that clung bewitchingly to hair and clothes. Deep-cushioned sofas beckoned on every side. Tall, opalescent windows glimmered with reflected moonlight. In the distance we heard the tinselly music of violins and laughter.

Though attired in his flannel nightshirt and patently fresh from sleep, desk clerk Marcel Dupres welcomed us as cheerfully as if this were not the dead of winter, the middle of the night, and the end of the line. Throwing on pants and mukluks, he escorted us jauntily over moon-dappled snow to our private chalet.

Here at last we found the stuff honeymoons are made of. Lamplight danced from satiny paneling and winking, beveled windowpanes. A single rose nodded magically from a milk-glass vase. Shortly two mugs of hot buttered rum were delivered to our door by the genie Marcel. We savored our drinks by a window draped in stalactites and cascading stars while a trio of radiators hissed and sang with the reassuring sounds of steam heat.

Overcome by relief, exhaustion, warm feet, and gratitude, I fell blissfully asleep on Ken's broad, toasty shoulder. (It was the last wholly carefree moment I was to have for years.)

I had arrived at Mont Tremblant with a trunkful (in those days few people traveled by plane and never with less than a full-sized steamer trunk) of lacy peignoirs and Carole Lombard lingerie, which I never unpacked; with two sets of L.L. Bean long johns, which I shortly wore twenty-four hours a day except for showers; and with a lot of illusions that were shortly shattered, among them the idea that I would learn to ski under my husband's loving tutelage.

"Martie," announced Ken after a breakfast that would have felled Man Mountain Dean, "meet André, your ski instructor."

"Sharmed, madame," said André, his tilted smile not unlike William Holden's.

"Oh really?" I heard myself chirruping in the idiot tones of the blue-nosed wombat. By the time I'd regained my composure it was to find that Ken had melted up the mountain with three Dartmouth boys and I was enrolled in the Johnny Fripp Ski School.

"Zair h'ees time before zee class, h'eef madame would l'ak zee short tour," said André, gallantly proffering an arm.

Lord, I'll admit it. Those were the Camelot days of skiing. There was an unstudied elegance about women attired in baggy pants, padded shoulders, and twenty-seven stripe beaver coats. (Women you just knew had never in their lives rushed to a grocery store because they were out of milk.) Old-world charm, unobtrusive money, and courtly manners were the rule. Since two dozen paying customers represented a banner day in any ski school in the world, each of us was handled like precious Lalique. Everyone dressed for dinner and then danced to the beat of a band with at least three saxophones.

I experienced a foretaste of this as I clung to André's arm and simpered shamefully, "Please call me Martie," meanwhile attempting to glide, not clump along in cumbersome, steel-tipped D'Artagnan boots. This feat was doubly difficult since André, like most Frenchmen, was a head shorter than I. I also made furious mental shopping notes, as it was immediately apparent that Mary Sachs of Harrisburg, Pa., may have known her Anne Fogartys but didn't know beans when it came to ski wear. In my windsock hood, shiny gabardine pants, and narrow-shouldered wool parka, I felt as tacky as a bag of dust rags.

Mont Tremblant was a self-contained village with its own boutiques, chapel, beauty salon, infirmary, restaurants, and bars—everything a girl could want with the exception of an added fifty degrees Fahrenheit. Even with the sun doing its damnedest, that entire end of Canada was colder than a week in Siberia. A vital part of the instructor's daily routine was to be on the alert for frozen flesh. "You in the yellow parka!" "Also zair in zee red cap!" they would shout at intervals throughout the day. "Frostbite on your left cheek . . . frostbite on zee nose . . ."

When one of them bellowed, "Attention in zee fonny parka, frostbite on your cheen!" I waved instant acknowledgment and stumbled off to the infirmary for first aid. "How can they tell?" I asked the nurse on duty.

"You develop white spots, usually on a protuberance like the nose or ears."

"I have a very firm chin. I should have known that's where I'd get it."

Soon I was up to my armpits in snowbanks and instructions, with no more time to mope about the degree of temperature, the state of my dress, the trembling of my thighs, or the hurt on my chin.

Our beginners' class was typical of beginners' classes everywhere. We looked like a fricasee of illegal immigrants in scruffy native dress as we shuffled from ski to ski and nervously eyed our leader.

André got right down to basics: how to wax our skis with red, blue, or silver, according to the coldness and texture of the snow; how to fasten our rumpled boots in their bindings, a process akin to baiting and setting a pair of bear traps; how to sling seven feet and forty pounds of hickory skis into the air and over the shoulder for transporting; where to purchase lift tickets; and, when the time came, that we would need a very warm coat for the chair.

The chair, I learned, was not electric. In lieu of electrodes it was fitted with a swinging bar to keep the rider from plunging headlong into the nearest abyss. As for the lift coat, it had better be warm. At a mean temperature of twenty below and a lift speed of an eighth-of-a-mile per hour, the early ski lift was an invitation to futuristic cryogenics.

When you reached the top, you staggered off, flexed your numb extremities and threw your lift coat onto a descending chair. From there the coat jounced solo to the foot of the mountain, where an operator casually tossed it onto a long wooden fence that daily held a cool million in mink, sable, beaver, and lynx. What's more, the coat was waiting when you skied down to retrieve it. Thievery in those primitive times was as inconceivable as breaking the sound barrier or entering outer space.

It was just as well I didn't know right away how little I was to see of my bridegroom: for breakfast and dinner, or as a passing blur on the Flying Mile. By the time this sobering fact dawned on me, I was too far gone to care. Years of athletic endeavor had done little to prepare me for the torturous demands of this deviant sport in a cruel and unnatural environment. (Right here is as good a time as any to confirm all suspicion that a skiing honeymoon is not conducive to idle billing and cooing.)

"Serves you right, darling," I droned nightly as I slumped into bed and asleep in a heady cloud of Sloan's Liniment.

The only thing that kept me going was André, who was in his first year as a ski instructor, and very young and very dear. He was also eager, earnest, devoted, and enduring.

"Allo, madame, zee boot she must be in zee toeplate," he would explain cheerily as I plunged out of my skis and into an adjacent snowbank.

Sunnily he repeated, "Non, non, Martee, to walk on zee skis you leeft first one, z'en zee othair. Watch André. I show you wahnce more."

After a barely audible sigh, he'd say gently, "Zee how-you-call-heem derriere, you tuck h'eem een, not h'out."

Like every fatuous young matron who has fallen a little in love with her obstetrician or tennis instructor, I gritted my teeth and tried.

Each morning Ken bounded athletically from beneath the blankets while I crept out of bed like a wounded infantryman inching his way across a minefield. Just bending over required Herculean will, and bending over was absolutely essential in order to pull on two sets of underwear, four pairs of socks, and one ponderous pair of ski boots. That accomplished, only a hefty assist from Ken straightened me up again. Then I fumbled into multiple layers of outerwear and at last staggered forth like the Tin Woodman to face another day of icy air, iron-booted feet, André's heart-wrenching smiles, and that odious muscle wrencher, the snowplow.

In those "olden days," as our children refer to them while their father and I brush the lint from our coats of chain mail, the path to the perfect snowplow was more menacing than an artillery firing range. Not only did we need true grit to clamp seven-foot, forty-pound skis in a tortured V-for-victory, we also had to plow our way bodily through rock-hard snow that was rutted to our calves. Mountain grooming, along with moonwalking, belonged to some unforseeable future.

Arlberg, I discovered, was no beer. It was an Austrian ski technique that was a purported improvement over the ancient telemark turn and the old one-pole-drag method. But not much. Employing Arlberg, a skier alternately swung and flung his recalcitrant body in broad, slow-motion gyrations, hopefully forcing his skis to follow. Experts back then estimated that mastering Arlberg (or any skiing whatsoever) required the same amount of time as earning a graduate degree.

After days of preliminaries in the snowplow and beginning Arlberg, André finally deemed our class ready for more advanced terrain. At last one morning he announced dramatically that all seven of us (two Hungarian countesses, two six-year-olds who were largely invisible under their mufflers, one lardy preppy from Lawrenceville, an ill-starred stockbroker, and me) were fit to come down from the top of the mountain. I was jubilant, to say nothing of André, who was sick to death of prodding us around the same dreary old snowpatch.

The stockbroker took one shuddering look at the dizzying three-thousand-foot summit of Mont Tremblant and, with the Gabor girls in tow, retired to the nearest bar. The rest of us rode endlessly on what seemed miles of chair, J- and T-bar lifts, up and up and up.

On arriving at the top of Tremblant for the first time, we tumbled to the ground like tenpins, brushed ourselves off, looked around and were promptly dumbstruck. In the ensuing years I have learned to live calmly with fourteen-thousand-foot peaks and panoramic, snowy vistas. Back then wintertime, mountaintop views were not easily come by. (None of us had ever seen one before.) "Wow," whispered an awestruck toddler through his muffler. "Technicolor," breathed another.

"She's magnifique, non?" said André, flinging his arms wide. She sure was. The cold had heightened colors so that the world had the jeweled quality of a Maxfield Parrish painting. Alders and birches were frozen in sugar plum poses, their branches graceful arcs. Evergreens marched across the mountainsides in snow-capped, military precision. An electric blue tent of sky rippled overhead. Below us minuscule skaters glided in parentheses of color across a doll-sized lake. I had to pause to catch my breath.

When I came to attention, it was to hear André say, "*Maintenant*, we take zee Nansen Trail. Zee trail she ees beginnair. You will l'ak heem." (André confused his genders in much the same way I did my left and right ski.) Dutifully we turned and pointed ourselves downhill.

The details of my progress down that mountain escape me today. I only recall that, once off my familiar snow-patch, I shattered like a piece of dropped Limoges. I fell down and apart on every slight turn, rise, dip, and short schuss of that easy little old Nansen Trail. After untold numbers of eggbeaters, as they're known in the trade, my brains were so scrambled I couldn't see or think straight. The two tots, their eyes bulging in alarm over their scarves, took turns heaving me to my feet. The Lawrence-ville kid put as much distance between us as humanly possible. It was humbling to know that, single-handedly, I had destroyed André's cheerful equanimity.

"Martee, ees it you forget? 'Ave I not show you *correctement?*" His voice was anguished as he cried, "So good you do heem down below."

Days passed. I fell. André grew morose.

"Ken, we might as well face it," I said shakily one night as I pried open a new bottle of Ben Gay. "I'm a washout."

"Maybe we should move you to another class," suggested Ken unhelpfully. Like any callous male who'd learned to ski in the days of jar-rubber bindings and self-help, he knew nothing about instructor worship.

"Never!" I howled, flinging myself disconsolately across a hot water bottle, two ice bags, three liniment jugs, and our Beefeater gin. "André would think he's a failure."

Ken picked up my discarded, rumpled ski clothes and said bleakly, "Maybe we should have tried Bermuda after all."

André persevered and so did I, but it was taking a lot out of both of us. Then one day he halted in the middle of the now-despised little old beginner's Nansen Trail, drew close and peered searchingly into my startled brown eyes. "Martee, ees it perhaps you cannot see where hees you go?"

Well, all those years of haunting libraries, reading in

bad light and getting high marks had taken their toll. Since high school I had groped myopically through gym classes, swim meets, and houseparty weekends—anywhere that glasses might hinder my social life, cramp my style or shatter and blind an eye. Contact lenses, along with color TV, were being tried out in New York and Chicago but were not yet available in the hinterlands. It just never occurred to me that anyone would wear glasses for something as dangerous as skiing.

André assured me, "But eef you can see, *chérie*, you weel no fall down."

I pulled out my spectacles, scraped the hoarfrost from my lashes and started again from the beginning. I still rumbled downhill with the grace and speed of a broadwinged pterodactyl. But at least I was under shaky control and largely upright.

I ventured off the Nansen and out onto Ryan's Run and the Tascherau. I even followed, however faintheartedly, in Iglook's tracks down the Flying Mile. André beamed and chattered and displayed me as his prize failure made good. As for Ken, he was relieved to know that both of us wouldn't have to give up skiing forever.

The Inn's other guests behaved like parents of a backward child who's finally mastered his two-wheel bike. I was showered with praise, treated to drinks and welcomed to the most select aprés-ski circles. I basked in the warmth like a spy who's come in from the cold.

At that exact moment European mountain men were streaming into the United States with battle-scarred skis on their shoulders and peacetime conquests in mind. New ski areas would soon dot New England hillsides. Better skis would be invented. Plastic and foam would revolutionize boots. Several thousand miles away in an old Colorado mining town, a handful of carefree souls were hiking up the massive mountain rising from their streets and then skiing back down. The first chairlift had not yet been built in Aspen, but people were beginning to visualize it.

Meanwhile, on the billowy, softly contoured sides of Mont Tremblant, I had discovered the lure of winter sun, frost-festooned air, lapis lazuli skies, and days that made the heart leap and the mind glow. Sometimes, in the joy of swooping down a ski mountain, I even forgot to grit my teeth.

What with one thing and another, it would be years before I got around to the beaches of Barbados or Bimini. My life and hard times in the ski world were about to begin.

* CHAPTER 3

Gingerbread
and Thermopane

KEN'S AND MY marital relationship had started to jell. We
had madcap personalities, a thirst for bold venture, and
a mutual aversion to budgeting. We were about as prag-
matic as the Bobbsey twins.

Possibly I should have been perturbed when Iglook
started talking about going into the ski business. And I
did make a few last-ditch appeals for sea and sand; but
mine was a voice bleating in the wilderness. After Ken
thoughtfully itemized the fortune we had sunk in my
Mannlicher boots, bear-trap bindings, laminated skis, and
André of Montreal ski suit, I threw in the beach towel for
good. The clincher was his studied observation, "I think
you'll graduate from snowplow turns to stem christies in
maybe a year or two, babe." Staggered by the force of
such encouragement, a woman is bound to grow light-
headed and lose perspective.

Listen, I was no more eager than Iglook to live a staid
and ordered existence. If the man wanted to pursue skiing
as a life's work, I would develop reindeer-hair armor and
join in the chase. I had no other plans, and it's not every
day you marry a man with more one-liners than Bob
Hope; who bakes hot blueberry muffins for breakfast; at-
tracts animals and small children; has greenish eyes and

22

good health; and looks ravishing in plumes and chain mail.

Let me only remind you that a generation ago skiing was not for the meek. It required inordinate amounts of cold blood, raw courage, arctic endurance, and economic sacrifice and had a very small (albeit fanatic) following. In its infancy, the sport was downright lethal. Not only that, just battling one's way to a resort or up a ski mountain required the bravado of a bullfighter.

We had gone straight from our honeymoon to Hanover, New Hampshire, which was a perfect location for young couples who skied and drank. America was moving away from wartime ersatz shoe leather and gas rationing, but on very leaden feet. In Hanover one could reach ski areas on a single gas coupon and one's social life within easy walking distance.

Ken found work as an oil company salesman. But since his morale, his supplies, and his salary were all very low, it was up to me to finance our continuing ski program. I painted an apartment house until the landlord ran out of paint and patience; wrote continuity for an eighty-watt radio station; washed up after the Dartmouth president's wife's Thursday teas; baked and sold Indian puddings and in evident desperation designed and sewed a voluminous hostess gown for a local grande dame from a bolt of ten-inch-wide contraband Japanese silk. I also had the leading role in a Green Hat production of *Arms and The Man*, but it didn't pay. On weekends I surfaced with coatimundi circles under my eyes attesting to my dozens of jobs, minimum wages, and shortage of sleep. We skied, but it was hand-to-mouth and from day to day.

Meanwhile, we had begun our search for ski slopes to call home.

I don't mean to sound ungracious about the birthplace of our nation, but in those days New England ski areas were as primitive as Plymouth Colony. And I noted that the owners' wives in all the farmhouses-turned-ski-hostelries looked as careworn as those pioneer women standing in front of Nebraska sod houses in 1876.

Then Iglook began to speak in spirited tones of the West, where he'd heard the mountains scraped the sky, the ski runs were wider than Paris boulevards, the snow was twenty feet deep on the flat, and as in Dixie the sun really shone all the time.

After several New Hampshire winters of rising in the morning to break the ice in our bedroom water pitcher and smile numbly through teal-blue lips as Iglook peered out at another bleak sky, beat his chest and bellowed, apparently from force of habit, "Man, what a beautiful morning!" I at least thanked heaven he was talking Out West instead of Far North. If he had pointed us toward Baffin Bay, in the direction of his ancestral roots, I believe my blackened, shriveled body would be resting today along some distant frost line.

As it happened, Daddy died of a coronary and Ken was hastily drafted into tires and retreads. Naturally, I considered our return to Pennsylvania on a par with indentured servitude on a polar expedition.

This doesn't mean that, other than intermittent lapses like having our first four children and building a flat-topped, gun-turreted house that looked like the Merrimac, we were ever really deterred. We refortified ourselves with short ski trips to the Poconos and long letters to every Chamber of Commerce along the Continental Divide.

Every few months we unfolded our dog-eared lists of improbable dreams, the Atlas road maps, and ski resort brochures and lovingly patted them smooth again.

Then fate turned up in the guise of that quiz contest.

I can't for the life of me remember what years the children were born, but for some reason I retain funds of minutiae such as the dates Ross edited *The New Yorker* and where the Ryukyus are. Looking back, I can see where my encyclopedic mind dampened a whole lot of well-planned dinner parties. But it also beefed up our cash flow and enabled us to balance the budget for the first time in our marriage. After that we parried the children's requests for pony carts and apologized to total strangers for not making them large loans. Then we packed our bags to go look at ski mountains.

Thinking us off for some lightsome R & R, Mother said solicitously, "A nice rest and a change will be good for you, darlings." Then in that undertone of disapproval perfected by mothers everywhere, she added, "Only I never heard of driving right up to the Rocky Mountains in all that ice and snow." Mother had seen the Grand Canyon in June, the California redwoods in July, the Yellowstone National Park in August. This was her idea of the only reasonable way to view the American West outside of a stereopticon.

I explained again that there weren't even any trains to some of the places we were going.

"And no mail, telegraph, or telephones, I gather." So far as Mother was concerned, skiing was the pursuit of mental deficients. But she was a good sport and had agreed to oversee the children, dogs, and Fanny Whitfield—who chewed snuff and helped me diaper the babies and dust in corners—or we wouldn't have made it across the nearest state line.

After double-checking the martini pitcher, bottles of olives, gin, and vermouth, our triple-zippered arctic sleeping bags, Coleman stove, antifreeze, boots, and skis, we gave the children an extra hug all around. Then feeling a little like Lewis and Clark, we pushed off for that country roughly bordered by Santa Fe, New Mexico, and Snoqualmie Pass in Washington.

We never made it past Aspen, Colorado.

Aspen is located on the western slopes of the Colorado Rockies, deep in the heart of six sockdolager ranges. It lies not only amid a large jumble of mountains, but also on the easternmost reaches of the Utah desert lands. Within an area of a few square miles, Aspen and its environs run the gamut from Sonoran desert vegetation to subarctic alpine tundra. One can climb from cactus country to glacier lilies in a day, and in summer the countryside swarms with over-stimulated botanists.

In the fifties the wintertime drive from Denver to Aspen required from five to twelve hours, depending on the whims of lurking avalanches and the number of ditched flatlanders snarling traffic. It featured such highlights as cloud-cloaked passes, a Colorado River canyon to make Bryce hunker down in shame, two-lane roads that twisted sinuously upward like sidewinders, and a surfeit of very high, terrifying scenery.

It was not until this first encounter with Colorado that I realized the extent of my acrophobia. A girl who had stared roller coasters, the Washington Monument, and Mont Tremblant fearlessly in the eye, I was taken aback to discover that I was unable to gaze forcefully over the edges of the Rockies. The heights dizzied me, my stomach tilted, and the true meaning of "mountainous" hit me head on. I spent most of the trip averting my eyes and gripping Ken's femur down to the marrow.

We drove into Aspen with a fiery sunset hot on our heels, Ken's right leg partially paralyzed for life, and me hyperventilating into a brown paper bag. Fortunately the town is situated on a broad mountain valley floor. Although at eight thousand feet, the sensation is that of a strong castle keep, with stalwart turrets, and towers of mountains rising to meet the sky. Thus comforted, I regained my senses and straightened my wimple.

In the late fifties Aspen was a leftover silver camp recently reborn as a ski resort. We had read in our brochures that men from the U.S. Tenth Mountain Division had trained nearby in World War II, discovered Aspen's magnificent terrain and returned from fighting in Italy to rebuild the town, install a few lifts and open a ski school. We knew that there were pretensions to culture, with a music festival and think tank planted and flourishing in the summer. And that Aspen's chief mentor and bank-roller was tycoon Walter Paepcke, owner of the Container Corporation of America and many high-minded concepts about *mens sana in corpore sano.* Our idea exactly.

I believe that we'd expected Aspen to resemble a Kitz-bühel travel poster. What we found looked more like a Ronald Searle drawing of winter in Marrakesh.

The snowy, unpaved streets were wider than Laredo's, and we wove dazedly through an architectural mélange of strawberry, lemon, and lime houses garnished with swirling catwalks, cupolas, and gazebos. Just as we de-cided the place was as Victorian as a buttonhook, we passed clumps of abandoned, silver miners' shacks and came smack up against early Bauhaus and late Mitzuko.

"Schönberg." I gurgled. "An atonal symphony . . . gin-gerbread and thermopane." Which smashing witticisms Ken was too staggered to notice. "Good Lord," he said at last. "Everyone in this town sure has a mind of his own."

We wound slowly through luminous pink evening blush we later learned was alpenglow. Before dusk settled over the castle keep, we had just time for a few choice vi-gnettes: a Greek garden planted in marble; a Charles Ad-dams mansion serving as a hospital and, we felt certain, as an incentive to speedy recoveries; a down-at-the-heels railway station, which had been appropriated by an in-terior decorator (who, it was rumored, flagged down the once-weekly train with swatches of batik); a church housed in a thirteenth century armory with bartizans and battlements; houses painted Cobalt blue and peacock green, magenta with pink, and yellow with bitter orange, and all gussied up in ironwork lace. The county court-house defied period definition. Its statue of justice was not even properly blindfolded. We finally stumbled into the Hotel Jerome to find the place done in Bernhardt-

Modjeska with flocking up the walls, nudes in the bar, and Cantonese bamboo housing the liquor.

Iglook and I waded through drifts lighter than popovers. Then we settled into a cheap but comfortable studio, where we felt as twittery as unmarried lovers. We held hands, sipped martinis and peered unbelievingly at storybook streets dusted artistically with fresh confectioner's snow.

Looming above the Aspen valley catchall of Victoriana, Taliesin High, and Dotty Dimple Swiss chalets rose a backdrop of mountains that would have brought Rudolf Bing to his knees. Anyone reared with the worn profiles of the Presidentials and sagging dewlaps of the Appalachians is simply unprepared for these muscular young colossi. Keep in mind that there are fifty peaks in Colorado over fourteen thousand feet, and that your average Alp stops dead around eight thousand, and you'll have some idea of what I mean.

Aspen Mountain rises straight out of the town, its heights so lost from view that one must stand back from far down valley to glimpse its summit. Up close, its hulking biceps and shoulders imply they could, if they wished, brush you off with the flick of a snowslide. Known locally as Ajax, Aspen Mountain towers over the south of town so that everything on that side of Main Street lies deep in its shadow from very early, on winter afternoons.

Having been tunneled and mined and prodded for gold, silver, lead, and zinc in a bygone century, Ajax has achieved lofty, Brobdingnagian aloofness. It has endured rough and ready mining men who packed their families and belongings up its face and built a thriving community in its cloud cover. Where skiers today follow the Buckhorn cutoff to Tourtelotte Park, a thousand people once looked haughtily down Ajax's nose at the hurly-burly of Aspen below. They even built aerial tramways to carry ore buckets and commuters, precursors of the latter-day chairlift. Today all of this is gone without a trace, no more than a wrinkle on Ajax's craggy visage.

On the north edge of town, Smuggler and Red Mountains are comparative molehills worn down by hot sun and high winds. Red Mountain is an eagle's aerie of cliff-hung homes that in heavy blizzards are reached by four-wheel drive or not at all. To the southwest, Highlands Peak, soaring Pyramid, and the Maroon Bells rise in jagged isolation. The Sawatch Range on the east is a ganglion of peaks marking the Continental Divide, that western watershed from which all headwaters flow east to the Gulf of Mexico or west to the Pacific Ocean. Up a valley carved millenia ago by a series of earth-moving glaciers, via the only wintertime exit from Aspen, flows the Roaring Fork River, its branches tumbling out of the encircling arms of Hunter, Snowmass, and Burnt Mountains. Beyond, like distant neighbors, the Elk, Collegiate, and other central Rocky Mountain ranges sprawl in tiered and snowy splendor.

One good look around, and we knew why the place was crawling with homesick Swiss.

Having been sired by an alpenstock, Iglook was panting to take on these mountains. His damsel, she of the faint heart and rumpled wimple, was not. I may have been smitten with the town. I was not enamored of ski terrain that looked like the Empire State building with curves.

At length I swallowed a fistful of Drarnamine, boarded the Number One lift and tucked my head in my parka front like a nesting duck. In the course of the hour's ride to the peak, we changed chairs and direction a number of times. I made the entire trip with my eyes either shut or clinging to the skyline, never daring a downward look. When we reached the summit, Iglook let out a whoop of exultant glee. I gazed down from 11,380 feet and wondered moodily if I would reach bottom again in this lifetime.

Since Ajax is layered like an immense, ornate wedding cake, I couldn't actually see bottom from up there. After Ken girded my loins and cajoled me into a few tentative runs, I was even lulled into a nice false sense of security.

The gentle dips and turns of Silver Bell, One and Two Leaf, and other notorious little shills plying the top layer of that mountain sucker the credulous into believing that all is safe as a church.

Late in the afternoon it was time to head for the bottom. Spurred on by my successes above, I took a deep breath and plunged downhill as if into a cold morning shower. It was then, along with Magellan's men, that I knew the world was dropping out from under me. Ruthie's Run, Copper Bowl, Elevator Shaft, every last trail down the turreted front of Ajax is listed as expert. And out west when we say expert, we *mean* expert.

After I had followed Ken onto a trail known as the F.I.S. from which there was no turning back, every expert descent I'd made to that date faded into lily-livered insignificance.

Ken was beside himself with joy. I was beside myself with horror and, hanging by mittened fingernails from a mogul top, I croaked, "Kenneth Robinson Sterling, you have br—brought me here to die."

"Will you just look at that view, sweetheart," he raved.

"I c—can't. I might fall off."

"For Lord's sake, Martie, you're not dangling from a thirty-story window. It's only a ski mountain. Stop acting like Harold Lloyd."

"Ken, I am in no sh—shape for levity," I pleaded. "I am paralyzed. Frozen fast. You've got to help me out of here."

Even Ken recognizes a case of nerves when he sees one and, with the assistance of two patrolmen who were clearing the slopes in the final sweep of the day and could not go home for dinner until I was safely removed, he wheedled me into inching my way, snail-like, to the bottom.

The Son of the Far North had directed me onto a run cut expressly for international racing and one that even today I am not inclined to ski. (I have never set foot on it again.) We had learned in short order that Iglook was a match for these mountains, but that I was not—a truth that has become increasingly self-evident over the years.

We also learned, like thousands of others, that life between eight and twelve thousand feet requires gradual acclimatization, and that skiing through thin air all day and running around meeting hundreds of people at nights was not the path to perfect health.

After that we took time to savor Aspen slowly instead of trying to gulp it in oversized bites. We sat back and gawked at mountains as overpowering as oceans. At a town full of broad greenswards and wide open space. At a blazing sun that vaulted daily over Smuggler Mountain and down into town. At a sliver of moon that hung delicately on the edge of the sky so as not to interfere with the sequined display of stars.

Like kids in a penny candy store, we were scarcely able to choose what we relished most: chairlifts floating disembodied against a crackled willowware sky; corrals, mine tipples, and Chic Sales attesting to the fact that this was indeed the storied West; *pâtisseries, badstus,* and *bierstubes* with their aura of old Vienna; a velvet, plush, and gilt opera house where we puffed up three flights of stairs to take in a Buster Keaton revival; Tompkins Hardware, with its musty air of decades past and stock of sadirons, miners' picks, and mule collars. Irrigation ditches still skirted the main streets. And we were told that cattle and sheep drives, which local wags sometimes detoured through the Jerome lobby, moved to and from the mountainsides in spring and fall. All of which gave one the feeling that Aspen had missed the turning of the century.

Finally we got around to peering over the edges of a two-million-acre national forest that was reportedly teeming with wildlife. "What kind of wildlife?" I wondered neurotically but not out loud. I may have had no head for heights, but if there were wanton bears and moose about, I planned to arm myself to the teeth and meet them head-on.

Visually surfeited, we agreed that we were crazy about the place.

We were here in January and could see for ourselves that the January thaw was a stranger to this paradise. There was enough snow to blanket all of Rhode Island, with fresh powder daily for breakfast. At the same time the sun was so cordial we skied in one sweater and a few layers of Coppertone.

The ski trails were an unexpected plus. It's true that plenty of them were steeper than haymows. But they were also broader than wheat fields, and we cowards could traverse them with the broad, sweeping cuts of a scythe. Eastern trails twisted like bobsled runs amid dense crowds of trees. Ken loved the challenge, but I'd always felt trapped in headlong flight to the bottom, with nowhere to turn.

Location? Aspen was no snap to get to. But neither were we somewhere north of Skagway. The town was on its way to having the busiest small airport in the country. And the Aspen Stage (a euphemistic term for the local bus line) regularly met trains at Glenwood Springs forty miles distant.

Construction of a well-equipped, twelve-bed hospital was in the offing, although it was distressing that the Addams mansion, built by rheumatism-racked miners in 1891, would have to go.

The schools were progressive and attracted bright young teachers from Haverford to Heidelberg who loved skiing and liked kids.

The summer season was rapturously described as a compote of good music, lofty thinking, and superb wilderness. Even though Ken was making suspicious noises about pack trips and running horses, it all sounded less ominous than I'd feared—chock-full of art, poetry, music, backpacking, trout fishing, in fact so much lust for life we wondered in passing when there was time to sit around and sulk. The answer is: during the interminable muds of spring.

Heaven knew there was a plethora of fascinating people, half of whom we'd already met on the run. A lot of them were newcomers who, like us, had surrendered to the razzle-dazzle of sunshine, scenery, and what they believed was heaven on earth. We were no dumber than the other patsies as we soaked up superlatives and Sure Tan instead of priming for life at hard labor. Or when we began pricing real estate instead of streaking for the nearest highway.

We had found our ski slopes to call home. The question was, how would we make a living? Aspen's career possibilities, short of prospecting for silver or raising legs of lamb, were decidedly limited. Searching for answers, we began totting up our assets. (I deigned not to reply when Ken said, "Too bad all yours are frozen, baby.")

Preceding and immediately following the births of the children, I had contributed five thousand hours of free labor to the Junior League—roller skating with the inmates of the State Hospital for the Insane and snapping pictures of unsightly newborns in a local maternity ward to raise money for birth control; I had had brief bouts of writing for *Mademoiselle* and the Harrisburg newspaper; operated a casually unprofitable little decorating shop; headed two United Fund campaigns; written, produced and directed five musical comedies that paid for a town library wing; and taught swimming to a long line of terrified housewives. I figured we wouldn't count house-breaking children or dogs or the fact that I'd matched the Yale laboratory record for nights without sleep (training which was to prove absolutely priceless). Ken surveyed me and my "accomplishments" with such weary disdain that it was evident he felt he should have given our marriage more thought.

Ken had steered family tires and retreads through bull and bear markets and camelback shortages. He'd proved a loving father, although his attentions ran to slapdash diaper changes, on-the-run hugs, and absentmindedly catching nonswimmers as they plunged off the country club diving board. He had seldom allowed paternal duty to interfere with his tennis games or directors' meetings. And he had given entirely too much of the children's and my time to the Pennsylvania National Horse Show, borough council quorums, sales conventions, Kiwanis luncheons, Masonic dinners, golf tournaments, inventorying, and volunteer work that ran neck and neck with mine. He was an ebullient host, an accomplished singer of libidinous songs, and an all-conference good sport.

We decided so long as we didn't have to make bearnaise sauce or do our own wiring, we could tackle almost any line of work.

By Lord knows what wild, circuitous thought processes, we came to the laughable conclusion that we were perfectly qualified to own and operate a ski lodge.

✳ CHAPTER 4

''Wagons Ho!''

WE STARTED off looking at five-unit motels that were sell-
ing for ninety thousand dollars and needed additions or
subtractions or both. We looked at cavernous Victorian
boarding houses with eighteen rooms, one bath, and wiring we suspected was circa 1888. After that we priced
empty city lots only slightly cheaper than Florida ocean
frontage. (If we'd had an inkling of their price twenty years
later, we would have held up a train and bought out the
town.)

At length, on the verge of defeat and despair, we
slumped off to the Aspen Highlands.

The Highlands clung to the far edge of Aspen, the
White River National Forest, and delusions of unwar-
ranted grandeur. It boasted the world's longest double
chairlift, Stein Eriksen's Ski School, very few customers,
and not a single ski lodge. Eventually it would be surrounded by hotels, palatial homes, a bustling city park, a
handsome high school campus, and parking problems. But
not now.

When we first saw the Highlands the year it opened, it
was reached via a stretch of dirt road, a lot of empty
ranchland, and the city dump. Beyond lay only Lou and
Had Deane's T-Lazy-7 Guest Ranch, a long-established

35

dude operation so isolated that the Lindbergh family had vacationed there in blissful anonymity for years.

Only seven minutes from the heart of town, the Highlands smacked of Ah, Wilderness. And it was here that Ken found what he had had in mind all along: four untrammeled acres of Engelmann and blue spruce, lodgepole pine, aspen, trout streams, spouting springs, and Rocky Mountain rocks—all smack-dab at the foot of a practically private ski mountain. Here at last was Iglook's holy grail, an ideal summer as well as winter location, rich virgin soil, Cockaigne in Colorado.

The only thing all this rustic seclusion spelled for me was w-o-r-k. I felt like a lonesome *campesino* gazing mournfully over the Sangre de Cristo mountains while a big, burly straw boss informed me, "Wal, with a little muscle we oughta be able to level 'em by the end of the month."

When we settled on keeping an inn, what I had in mind was a cozy little ready-built chalet, fully furnished with beds and bedding, chintz curtains, leather hassocks, and pots and pans. I had never remotely entertained the idea of starting from scratch, beginning with our own lumbering.

Since most of the untrammeled acreage was over a very steep precipice and under ten feet of snow, we didn't exactly find it, either. I was in favor of borrowing crampons, pitons, and snowshoes and seeing what was *down* there. (I can tell you what was down there. A succession of beaver dams constructed along the lines of the Petersburg defenses, which it took us years of sweat and toil to untangle so we could drain off hundreds of square yards of bog and slime and dispose of, among other things, the eight-hundred-pound putrefying carcass of a cow elk, that's what was down there.) "Are you crazy?" was the way Ken put it and indicated the wide upper shelf of land where we would build our lodge.

"It's the perfect spot—well drained, and the timber isn't

too heavy. Those big spruces will provide great shade for our southern exposure. Later we can clean up the lower acreage for horse corrals and . . ."

"But Ken, *dear*, what about the expensive roads we'll have to build just to get down there?" I pleaded.

Ken's woodsy New Hampshire upbringing had overcome him, and he was blinder than a blinkered dray horse to every barrier I pointed out. "What about transportation for our guests?" "How about school for the children?" "Who puts out fires in wilderness areas?" "What will we do with . . . Ken? Ken?" I realized he was lost in reveries of dead growth, chain saw, axe, and hatchet. Years ago his mother had warned me, "He's inherited his father's passion for pruning, Martie. You'll have trouble hanging onto your rose bushes." Sure enough, he whacked off perfectly good branches of my favorite ramblers, exclaiming, "There, that'll fix 'em." It did, and they died.

I sighed inwardly, looked over expanses of tangled brush and fallen trees and came to the conclusion that he'd be so busy with the big, challenging stuff that I might grow some unmolested flowers.

Besides, there was nothing more I could say. (Oh, there was plenty more I could say, but not anything he would care to listen to.)

In a paroxysm of activity we swept around the valley locating a surveyor, an architect, and a contractor. Then, during a pitifully unceremonious encounter that left us flurried and flat broke, we signed a check that gave us title to our very own four acres of Rocky Mountain.

Back East we located a family who loved our unmarketable Merrimac house and induced them to buy it at a sizable loss to us, resigned from a total of twenty-seven dues-paying organizations and tearfully said good-bye to Mother and two of our three dogs. My brother Whit had by this time parted from a wife and a succession of housekeepers. He was already in Colorado, stamping out disease in Denver, so we added his two children to ours, thus bringing the sum total of kids to six, ages ten and under.

For the final move west we had two station wagons. But what we needed was a Mayflower van with built-in bunks, lavatories, laundry room, and a solitary confinement cell. By the time we had strapped on, in, and around the two cars the twelve suitcases, last minute laundry, ironing board, small antiques I simply could not trust to the movers, fishing rods, guns, cookies, picnic hampers, coolers, the Bachrach portrait of Mother, coloring books, crayons, the Monopoly set, beach towels, bathing suits, wet washcloths in plastic bags, thermos jugs, litter bags, our newest books and records, and the children, we looked like Ma and Pa Kettle en route to the Washington State Fair.

We knew we wouldn't be back this way, and it does make a difference.

Making the trip with Ken at the wheel and me clutching his tibia had been terrifying. Driving it myself was beyond my wildest imaginings. When we reached the Front Range of the Rockies, it was summer and we were able to travel shortcuts that did not circle decorously around the more vicious heights but instead went dead ahead and straight up. I became frantically aware of yawning canyons, sudden chasms, enormous reaches, and other dizzying sensations. I did not dare suggest that Ken tow me. And since it was only two o'clock in the afternoon, it was entirely too early to stop for the night. I had no choice but to carry on. Without the children I never would have made it. They sang lustily, told jokes and riddles and diverted me with vigorous conversation as we crossed deep unrailed arroyos.

As we hummed across the high, flat plateau between Leadville and Twin Lakes, I finally relaxed enough to burble, "Well, darlings, we're over Loveland and Vail Passes and all those great big mountains, and we must be nearly there." Our route was news to me. Ken had the road maps and the chutzpah, and I followed where he led. But we were no longer going uphill, and I considered this a good, healthy sign.

Then we started up Independence Pass, and like a woman in the final stages of labor, I knew I must go it alone.

Independence Pass is the principal shortcut from Denver to Aspen and is one of the highest traveled mountain passes in the continental United States. Even today, elegantly paved, it is open only in summer and known to reduce the most levelheaded middle-American motorist to jellied consommé. In those days it was unpaved, as twisted as a mad mind, narrower than string, and largely unloved. I didn't even know it was there.

We jolted abruptly off the macadam, onto a pock-marked dirt track, around a boomerang turn, through a monolithic stand of spruce, and for one brief, awful moment I glimpsed what looked like Annapurna and K-2 rising directly in our path. I shrieked at Ken, "Stop! Stop this minute," but he was engulfed in mushroom clouds of dust and flying rock ahead.

Foot frozen to the accelerator, I trailed in his wake. We turned and wound and climbed past crashing mountain streams, roaring falls, boulders the size of dreadnoughts, through monstrous thickets of fir, and beneath overhanging pinnacles of glacial moraine. The "road" eventually narrowed to the dimensions of a burro trail, so that we crept between sheer rock walls rising to our right and sheer rock cliffs dropping off to our left.

At length we reached the high point where the continent divides and there's nothing but you, infinity, indignant bighorn sheep, and no vegetation whatsoever because you are *one thousand feet above tree line* and only one step removed from hurtling into orbit. I felt just as though Mother Nature had heaved me on top of the world, reminded me not to fool with her and abandoned me, alone and unloved.

The children begged, "Mother, please don't cry. We're right here. Please don't cry."

"Stay where you are," I croaked.

They were on the floor of the car, where I had ordered them several light-years before. I didn't give a hoot in hell for psychologists' warnings about transference of fears to the young. I needed all the nerve I possessed just to maintain a viselike grip on the wheel with palms as clammy as oysters.

A quivering mass of protoplasm, I waffled behind the carefree, speed-mad Kenneth Sterling Moss down the other side of that divide at a murderous thirty-five miles per hour. On reaching our rental house, Ken scraped me out of the front seat, separated my frozen claws from the wheel, supported me indoors and poured my gelatinous body into bed.

Within fifteen minutes Dan, our youngest, appeared in the doorway holding a wild-eyed calico cat and announced, "Look, mom. Big bad wolf."

In a half hour Gwyn and Dede delightedly brought their new find, a small, startled female, to meet me. "She's our size and lives right next door," they exclaimed delightedly.

In forty minutes Whit and Mike presented me with a dead porcupine whose quills were blessedly in a state of flux.

And in forty-five minutes on the dot, Robin, the oldest, appeared at the door with her father grinning conspiratorially behind her. She rattled the martini pitcher, pranced with anticipation and inquired, "Mother, aren't you going to watch our beautiful sunset from our beautiful new front yard?"

I knew when I was defeated. The sunsets and the children win every time.

CHAPTER 5

The Wild In The West

IN THOSE prehotel management days, building a successful lodge business, with returning clientele, took youth,
ignorance, a Ouija board, and a good location. In the beginning we were also certain that a couple of college degrees, our cheery willingness to work, hot blood, passion
for skiing, and gregarious personalities would see us
through.

One by one we learned harsh, unpalatable truths. To
survive in early Aspen you needed apprentice training in
plumbing, heating, electricity, carpentry, masonry, welding, veterinary medicine, mountain rescue, automotive
mechanics, and wilderness survival. A law degree with
plentiful experience in water rights would have helped.
Also the constitution of a yak and the stoicism of a Ute
squaw.

One of the original thirteen prospectors who clawed his
way over Independence Pass and struck silver in 1879
wrote, "I stuck to the ranch for two years, fishing and
hauling hay, having a good time and a hard time and a
hell of a time all the time." Things have changed very
little. And mostly it's a hard time or a hell of a time all of
the time.

We started off smoothly enough, with Ken employed by our contractor as unskilled labor at two dollars an hour. The children were in school except for Danny, who with two new dogs and the calico cat contentedly stayed underfoot through long days of unpacking and sweeping up the leavings from the rental house's shedding wicker furnishings.

Between times I ran from window to window gazing rapturously at the view. Eventually I discovered that every last house in Aspen has a breathtaking view and this is something you accept as your due, like naturally curly hair.

Very soon, like a ragtag relay team, we were running as if wild horses were behind us. There was no time for vista viewing any more. The track grew faster as, nightly, contractor John McLaren and Ken and I settled over reams of paper and pots of coffee, after the children were tucked in bed, and worked out building details one day ahead of the oncoming workmen.

Our architect had designed a simple building: a two-story parallelogram bristling with cedar shakes, native spruce, and used brick—the whole to lie along the edge of our sloping site overhanging Maroon Creek. This gave us a split-level effect. The front of the lodge buried its chin in the ground. The backside bared expanses of glass to Buttermilk Mountain spiraling above; to grandfather spruces rising eighty feet in behemoth conversational groupings; and to the creek rushing noisily along one hundred feet below. This daily drama might not excite the older, more jaded playwrights, but it was almost more than we ingenues could endure.

From the center of our quadrangular building a cedar-shaked A-frame was to rise like a secular church spire ("Open the church and here are the people"). This would be our guest lounge, the hub and heart of lodge life. Guest rooms were to be reached through, beyond, and beside the lounge via sheltered outside walkway/balconies. Our own apartment was buried at ground level, with dormitories and more guest rooms on each side. The creekside room views were of course spectacular, but the front had its share too. Every window and doorway would frame Highlands Mountain, its ski trails, and, we hoped, legions of colorful skiers.

The track grew bumpy when we first encountered the Reluctant Workman. John himself could not have been a more confirmed workaholic, as were most of his crew. But none of us had more than nebulous control over the so-called subcontractors (undoubtedly taken from the Old English for "subhuman").

I knew the track was getting too fast the night I overheard John complaining to Ken, "I'm not sure the plumbing boys have the right answer."

"The right answer to what?" I demanded from the sink where I was juggling coffee cups.

"They've decided to put an electric pump down by the springs instead of using a shallow well system," Ken explained.

"What springs?" I just hate being querulous, but it seemed to me that we were already depending too much on nature—like for sun and snow in the proper amounts at exactly the right moments. Any woman who's coped with rained-out reunions, windy wash days, or frozen power lines can tell you that Mother Nature is about as reliable as a female in postpartum depression. Not for the first time I reminded Ken, "We are building a ski lodge that must provide dependable facilities for paying guests who will expect to be warmed and watered in constant comfort. Now what was it about those springs?"

"Martie, this is something you simply won't understand."

"Maybe if you explain it, dear. What if these springs dry up?" (They haven't yet.) "What if they freeze in winter?" (Never did.) "What if the pump breaks down?" (Four times so far.)

Having grown to maturity among municipal water mains that chugged along pumping out millions of gallons of water from a secret source that was no concern of mine, I belonged to the school of thought that uncomplaining payment of your water bill was a privilege and a pleasure.

"We'll never have to pay another water bill as long as we live," Ken exclaimed jubilantly. The thought filled me with chill dread.

Other niceties of civilization we didn't have to pay for because we didn't have them were sewage disposal and fire protection. At first I fretted about these inadequacies, but gradually I ceased interjecting my neuroses, especially into anything falling under the nauseous heading of "man's work." After some mortifying misunderstandings about nipples and joints and elbows, I retired gratefully from the fields of plumbing and construction.

I was galloping like a colt in April, just to hold up my own end. The laundry alone was almost my end. Every couple of days I staggered to the town's lone, ill-equipped laundromat where I read year-old issues of *McCall's* while our mountains of dirty clothes sloshed around in chilly gray water and then, since the laundry had not seen fit to invest in dryers, lugged sixty-pound baskets of wet wash home to be hung up with clothespins.

"I didn't realize clothespins were still on the market," I said to Ken in disbelief.

"To say nothing of the shovel, the hoe, the wheel, and its barrow." Ken was as discouraged with his antediluvian work ethic as I was with mine.

The scrub oak burst into flame, alluvial fans of golden aspen fluttered against the great, dark breasts of the mountains, and the days slowly grew crisper. Out by the clotheslines I chased magpies, blew on my red chapped hands, recollected the peaceful purrings of my forsaken washer and dryer and tried to envision once again those dozens of comforting dials and adjustments. Before long they eluded me completely. I was busy maintaining eternal vigilance over the children and their clothes, steering them away from the loose dirt of irrigation ditches, compost heaps, and horse corrals. The children themselves never missed television for a minute. But their mother longed for an outsized Zenith console where she could chain them right after whipping the clean shirts off their backs to be worn again another day.

As molten aspens faded and the mountains dimmed to the tawny color of lions, running the track took on the nightmare quality of slogging through hip-deep hasty pudding. Between trips to the laundromat and the lodge site, I relaxed at the sewing machine, stitching in bad light far into every night. By the middle of December I had manufactured twenty-eight bedspreads, thirteen slipcovers, eighteen sets of draperies, twenty-two bed bolsters with covers, dozens of bright scatter cushions, uncounted lamp shades, and two enormous canvas log carriers. Shopping on a budget tighter than a fitted sheet, I was limited to purchases of cheap cricket chairs upholstered in Halloween muslin; to lamps with shades woven of cigarette paper; and to footstools covered in plastic Naugahyde. I bought them. But I ripped every last one apart and recovered them in bright, fresh fabrics. There were a number of things we had to splurge on, such as good mattresses and miles of handsome leather built-ins for the guest lounge. So where I could, I cut corners, costs, and slipcovers.

As I upholstered, fitted and pinned, I brooded over the dark and deleterious day I'd been a decorator and learned how to do these things.

Another of my duties as chatelaine of our emerging hostelry was publicity. Rose Crumpacker, secretary of our Chamber of Commerce, showed me the ropes and also the Chamber, a dumpy cement block building reminiscent of a Maginot Line bunker.

When an unsuspecting skier wrote a letter of inquiry to Early Aspen, he was laying himself open to the biggest avalanche of mail since the Nixons acquired Checkers. Every lodge owner in town met at the bunker, drank gallons of coffee, read the mail—which on heavy days amounted to twenty-five letters—and sent off stacks of literature, rate sheets, color postcards, and brochures, in an eager bid for the inquirer's attention. The mailbag offered many juicy tidbits from those unaware of our close communal association. For example: "Last winter we stayed at the Bide-A-Wee-While and did not like the place one bit." Naturally the rest of us added many cutting comments on the margins so the luckless proprietors of the Bide-A-Wee-Et-Al could read them and weep. Every innkeeper bore his or her share of the criticism. As Rose warned with a wry grin, "Get ready, Martie. Even though you're as cheerful as a Tupperware lady and more help than Travelers' Aid, someone will come to loathe you, or your beds, or your children, or . . ."

I chuckled in moronic disbelief, meanwhile putting aside those letters in which I detected a slight flurry of humor, so that I could write clever personal replies explaining why the charming Campbells would love our nutty establishment and style. And of course us, our beds, our children.

Ken and I, in rare contemplative moments, had agreed that the words "ski lodge" should conjure up firelight, cold cheeks, hot drinks, and the camaraderie of a great big happy house party. We knew what we liked, and we were dead certain the rest of the ski world would love exactly the same things. Naturally we foresaw shortcomings. Our office would be so small you'd have to enter it crablike. Some of our first guest rooms were not much bigger than oxygen tents, and as Ken put it, "People will have to go outside to change their minds." And then there was the little matter of geography.

Our new Aspen friends thought our location rotten and they said so. "You mean you're building way out there in the country?" they asked incredulously and often. I suppose, with Buttermilk Mountain barely open for business beyond us, and Snowmass only a glistening, empty mountain down valley, that we were an outpost of sorts. Despite the fact that Lou and Had Deane had operated T-Lazy-7 successfully for years, it was true that beyond them were nothing but raw mountain ranges, melting glaciers, and half-forgotten mountain passes. Still, Aspen Mountain, with a sum total of fourteen runs (albeit magnificent ones) was not, we felt, the be-all and end-all of local skiing. The Highlands offered fresh new terrain, was only a few minutes from town, and we were certain our flair for hospitality would outweigh the minor drawback of not being in the middle of traffic.

As I waxed more lyrical about the attractions of our happiness hotel, Rose kept warning, "You'd better get all this down in a brochure, my dear, and soon. Keep composing those long letters to perfect strangers, and you'll have writer's block by Christmas."

Our brochure couldn't be written until we'd settled on a name for the place. We were still undecided when Rose phoned to say, "I hate to pressure you, Martie, but the winter listing goes to press tomorrow and we must have a name for your place by noon."

This was worse than a twenty-four-hour ultimatum to name a baby or a battleship. And Ken was no help at all. He kept falling asleep, but by restoking him with cups of coffee, I kept him at it until three o'clock in the morning, when we settled wearily on The Heatherbed. It had a Scotch flavor to match the Highlands, as well as the comfortable air of "featherbed." Certainly it didn't lend itself to plagiarizing.

The Heatherbed at the Highlands made the listing by a hair, and our handsome brochures were soon ready at the *Aspen Times*. They were printed on egg carton paper and rumored to have reduced the typesetters to raving lunacy.

An actual brochure published in living color gave me a

comforting sense of "well done." Nevertheless, I felt absurd for a few months, sending out trilling panegyrics that described the beauty of our glass-walled guest lounge—still piled high with scrap and as unglassed as a bombed-out greenhouse; the grandeur of our twenty-five-foot fireplace—only half-bricked and virginal; the snug and cushy comfort of our guest rooms—presently bare-floored, with the air of an empty warehouse; and the spectacular view from every window—invisible through layers of paint, putty, spackle, and grime. When I got around to rereading this drivel in January, I was astonished to find it had all come true.

We forged ahead battling the wild in the West and the unpredictable in nature. Sometime in September before our second story was installed, we had an inclement early snow. Construction slowed while Ken, cursing mightily, shoveled two feet of slush from our future living room, dining room, kitchen, bedrooms, baths, the office, and four guest units.

The children were also, one by one, broken in with a bang. Having heretofore led sheltered lives around a well-guarded country club pool and decorous suburb, they were ill-equipped for life in the rough. One morning, neighbor Elizabeth Chamberlain carried Danny in from her front yard where a grazing horse had casually moved to one side and stepped on him, inflicting a sizable dent. Thus we learned that those quaint backyard corrals developed breaks faster than penny balloons, and that we were liable to find livestock in our pansy beds any old day of the week. One evening the house shook like tapioca pudding and we looked out to see an escaped herd of horses thundering across our lawn. After that we tightened security on the children. It seemed ridiculous to lose any of them in a stampede this late in the century.

I never feared for the kids' lives. But they had embarked on some very nerve-racking pastimes: exploring old mine shafts and prospect holes; fishing off precipitous embankments; swinging from vines over yawning canyons; riding half-wild burros bareback. What's more, they contrived to injure themselves in midweek when their Uncle Whit was not on hand. After a while I considered having him give me a course in home stitching to cut down on doctor bills.

In this frontier environment there were two clear-cut choices. I could gather the children to my bosom and clutch them there, in which case none of us would have lived life to the fullest. Or we could adapt. We adapted. The children finished their first school term scarred, chapped, battered, resourceful, and able to bear pain—a lucid reminder of their mother's combat-hardened childhood. Their father and I were proud of them.

In this same environment my eyes turned red from sewing, my hands red from wet wash, and not infrequently I yearned for bridge luncheons, social columns, and new hats, although back east I had detested all three.

The man of the house smashed new, untouched fingers weekly and had long ago lost the last of his excess pounds and executive pallor. Nightly we painted his blistered, bleeding fingers with tincture of benzoin, dressed the children's latest wounds and counted the hours until D-Day.

Our first guest reservations were for December twentieth, and by mid-November I began composing fey little notes of apology, just in case. John and his crew were working double time and overtime, but as the safety margin narrowed, the delays over wiring, heating, plumbing, and masonry only increased.

Our rental lease on Wicker Haven expired on November twenty-fifth and, ready or not, we ate Thanksgiving hot dogs on planks, sawhorses, and the damp cement of our new ski lodge. We were moved in. Our own roof was over our heads. But I can tell you I was not keen about roughing it amid piles of scrap lumber; or cooking for eight over cans of Sterno; or giving the younger children baths in the lone working sink where we were also soaking the dirty socks and underwear that we needed sometime before next year; or locating school clothes, mittens, coats, parkas, and hats in pyramids of boxes stacked among cases of Celotex and vinyl tile.

Since this was our third move in six months, I had lost complete touch with law and order. Despite all my earlier judicious planning, every last thing we owned was now misplaced. Each morning at school bus time and every evening at dinner and bedtimes, there was a tearful, frantic search for some vital piece of clothing or equipment, which left me putty-colored and trembling. We finally found the electric trains the autumn we moved out and Robin's stuffed bear the year she was twenty-five.

Our disheartening lists of vital things-to-be-completed seemed scarcely to shrink at all. Only Ken and I did. We worked ever longer hours, bolted down meals and lost weight until I pictured us draping ourselves in loose folds of flesh like Roman togas.

By December tenth the tinsmiths had not arrived to weld and install the sixteen-foot fireplace hood, which lay scattered in sections on our lounge floor like a dismembered brontosaurus. And in our apartment we were still pigging it amid piles of sawdust, nails, lumber, scrap, pegboard, blowtorches, workmen's lunch boxes, workmen, sawhorses, and rusting nuts, bolts, and screws.

We were, we found, at the doubtful mercies of the serviceman. The serviceman may not be an iota more reliable in the city. But in the city, when the electrician or plumber fails to arrive, you thumb through the phone book and eeny-meeny pick another. Here there wasn't any other.

When we had progressed far enough to do the heavy painting, every last painter in town had started ski clinics or instruction. In a frenzied talent search we finally turned up Keith Sawvel and Ed Cain. Keith and Ed were actually abstract expressionists, but as we maintained, "You can push a paint brush, can't you?"

The art market was at low tide and so were their funds, so they took us on. They were a godsend, very creative and not choosy about working hours. The later the hour, the harder they brushed. Often we were all slapping paint at two o'clock in the morning.

Living with us by this time were our first ski bums: Ellie Hurst, Jim Pomeroy, and Jim Jacobson.

Before going another step, I'd like to point out that "ski bum" conjures up false pictures of laggards, goldbrickers, and ne'er-do-wells. In truth it is a term of deep affection. The word *bum* when combined with *ski* meant courage and commitment. It meant tough, sinewy kids who had gambled on the trek to Colorado ski country, and were willing to mop floors, chop roof ice, change beds, muck out toilets, do anything short of kill for a ski pass.

As rough and tumble as ski bums were, neither were there any sveltely tailored, glossily manicured hotel managers in the early Aspen ranks. Employer and employee alike endured dishpan hands and the minimum wage and would have fallen to pieces around the likes of Leona M. Helmsley.

Most lodge owners were, like us, strictly nonprofessional—demented young couples with no more knowledge of hotel management than Robinson Crusoe. The mechanized hotel chain, with its exact duplication of service and decor in one hundred and thirty-seven cities, was not yet abroad in the land. Meanwhile we amateurs were inept, but we were lovable. And we tried harder.

Jim Pomeroy would go to work for Bert Bidwell at the Mountain Shop when the season started. He was temporary, but very welcome. He and Jake came to us fresh from Army duty in Europe where they had made a successful assault on the Russian exhibition building at the Brussels World's Fair. Not, however, in the line of duty. Jake was a connoisseur of quarts of sour mash washed down with light German lagers. Thus fortified, he had scaled the Communist showpiece with crampons and removed the hammer and sickle from under the noses of a Red Honor Guard who was being diverted by Jim with abnormal behavior on the ground. This was exactly the sort of derring-do our lodge would require. Looking back, I'm surprised more of our bums were not devout Christian Scientists.

Ellie was an O.R. nurse from Boston's Peter Bent Brigham Hospital, a copper-haired, skinny Hibernian who loved letting down her hair and slipping into her grandfather's brogue.

She announced to me the very first thing, "I'm sick to death of needles and banged noodles. I'd hate to tell ye what an overdose I've had."

"Well siree," I assured her in false, bright tones, "you've come to a healthy place. Our altitude does wonders for the lungs, and it's just perfect for people with oily skin who like to ski."

"Ah, heaven," sighed Ellie happily. Then she scowled. "But I want no one knowing I'm a surgical nurse. Or I'll be lookin' at tonsils and dispensin' medicines instead of breathin' fresh air and learnin' to ski."

Ellie's season with us stretched into a year. We would have liked to keep her around until the end of time. Not only did she cheerily tackle beds, breakfasts, bathtub rings, and total child care, but despite herself stanched more blood flow, applied more tourniquets, administered more shots and dressed more wounds than a lone medic on Pork Chop Hill.

With the help of subterfuge, and promises of everything from deathless devotion to free rooms for relatives, we finally coaxed every last workman into finishing his job. How he finished it was another story altogether. Over the coming seasons time would not only tell, it would squeal on every last piece of cheating in the Heatherbed lodge. We didn't know it then, but we didn't have long to wait before these revelations began.

Book II
DAYS OF
STEIN
AND ROSES

CHAPTER 6

Home For The Holidays

As CHRISTMAS approached and our first guests trickled picturesquely through the snow, Ken and I thrust aside dismal thoughts of meeting our Maker in lieu of our deadline. The air was filled with the scent of spruce boughs (almost but not quite pungent enough to stifle the odor of alkyd flat enamel), and we could have sworn we heard jingle bells just over the hill.

As the children tell the world, and I confess it's true, "Mother is a sucker for Christmas." It's a good thing. If I'd suffered from Yuletide depression, that was the year I might have hung myself from the nearest rafter.

Our offspring had been assured by friends that if God-given ponderosa pine or Colorado blue spruce did not grow in your backyard, you simply cut what you needed from millions of board feet of timber in the nearest national forest. With only a few backward glances to see if we were being shadowed, we gathered baskets of pine cones and garlands of evergreens that we draped across unfinished window frames, unpainted doors, and a few uncurtained windows. If a corner loomed empty, we smothered it in sprays of shiny kinnikinnick and groaning armloads of boughs. With our giant spruces snow-capped and stationed decoratively around the outside, and the interior littered with eighteen species of conifers, we were soon Christmas-cardy as all get out. Of course the lodge was a firetrap, but then I didn't expect lightning to strike until summer.

Just as we were hanging a beautiful gleaming holly wreath, a gift from Ken's mother, on our bright red lounge door, a providential heavy snowfall descended like a benediction and buried the ugly stacks of builders' debris dotting our grounds.

All things considered, we looked and felt as festive as a Christmas cover for *Town and Country*.

In the Mom-and-Pop hostelries of the days immediately preceding the great condominium takeover, the guests and their quarters came first. The owners' housing acted as catchall, disposal, and hide all—the untidy back pocket hidden behind the sparkling white shirt front of the inn. After our last room was filled and every guest comfortable, the sainted Jake and Ellie flatly refused my offer to take time off to ski. With one brief, longing glance at the mountain, they dispatched me for a long winter nap and pitched in to mop out the Augean stables we called Home. Working like hostelers, they scrubbed and polished our apartment. They handpicked a small family tree and covered it with popcorn, cranberry strings, and the children's homemade, unstylish tinfoil, egg-carton, gingerbread, and construction-paper ornaments.

I abhor disorder, and they couldn't have given me a grander gift.

Despite a workload that would have staggered a rickshaw driver, we'd also found wonderful friends. In the spot we were in, your best friends are the ones who are there soonest with the most help.

Ria Beyer discovered me in the post office back in September as I was materializing from another large, wet wash at the laundromat. She escorted me straight to her place for coffee, küchen, and a firm offer of friendship. Ria ran the Vagabond Lodge beautifully and efficiently while her husband Bill attended interminable city council meetings, worked for the Aspen Ski Corp. and operated the Wintershop. They'd come to this country when they were young and the world was between wars. By dint of very hard work, they'd built a prosperous life in Aspen. Ria answered my thousands of questions and abandoned her own busy lodge long enough to help me sort linens and scrub windows and to provide us with spaetzle, linzertorte, and sauerbraten, any one of which Ken would have crawled through burning coals for.

Connie and Otto Steiner of the Hindquarter Restaurant brought us trays of pastries and stayed to make beds. Elizabeth Chamberlain brought us a new English setter puppy named Heather and stayed to wash crates of dishes. Mariellen Powers and Sheila DeVore brought casseroles. Joan Metcalf scrubbed tubs until time to wash her own face, slap on some lipstick, rush off to the Crystal Palace and sing over people's suppers. George and Ginny Parker drove in from Denver to contribute weekend labor after George had slaved over a hot practice all week with Uncle Whit.

Caroline Clayton Calhoun Ethridge was pointed in our direction by an eastern friend who'd known her at Sarah Lawrence, causing Ken to growl balefully, "Tell your friends not to do us any more favors."

Claytie was early thirtyish, with a sleek mane of sunbleached hair, wicked peridot eyes, and the voice of a crazed frog. She was descended from a long line of oil wells and gilt-edged municipals, and at the time we met had been married to and divorced from a succession of men who'd each left her with fewer oil leases and less and less real estate.

She lived on day-old salad and twenty-year-old Scotch, on B-12 shots and turbulent love affairs. She painted in oils, played jazz piano, flitted from spa to spa, and drove her Mercedes 450 SL home to Tulsa for semiannual shopping sprees "charged to Mawsie, of course," and prattled on about my precarious perch directly on the Libra-Scorpio cusp. She had a very strong will and delightedly "took in hand" those of her friends she felt needed management. Unfortunately this soon included me.

When Claytie first appeared at our construction site looking smashing in Bernardos and a Lilly, with malachite cigarette holder, and a go-to-hell charm bracelet jangling with gold, jewel-encrusted charms, followed by a cat in sheep's clothing—a lhasa apso named Marzipan—and picking her way distastefully through piles of lumber, she was shocked to her manicured toes. She found me filthy, dishevelled, covered with stickers as thick as privy seals, on my back, scraping at a toilet base with jagged fingernails. "Like a charwoman, poor thing," she shuddered later.

For inexplicable reasons she did not flee. She didn't help. She hindered our progress. But she did not flee. I believe we may have held the same fascination for her that a snake has for its paralyzed prey.

From that day forward Claytie deplored, and sought to remedy, the state of my hair, my house, my hands, my wardrobe, and my sex life.

Claytie called Ken "Father" in deference to all those children, who secretly dismayed her, although she brought them thoughtful gifts from her many travels and taught them about witches and warlocks. "I'm an Arcturian, you know, children, and this is my second time around as a witch. They've asked me to serve another term, but I'm really rather tired," she would explain with weary otherworldliness to our round-eyed girls. When, after lying blessedly fallow for years, I later gave birth to Sarah Millard Sterling, Claytie became her godmother and presented her with an elaborate Haitian Voodoo kit. Eventually she introduced all the children to the mysteries of the libido, advanced bartending, penis envy, Frank Harris, Henry Miller, and downshifting. She gave any child old enough to see over the steering wheel a few peremptory driving lessons and immediately began sending him or her on errands. Ken was outraged, but the children all drove well at an early age, the local laws of those days were pretty casual, and soon he was dispatching them on errands himself.

So was I. When Whit was eleven or twelve, I found myself alone in the lodge with a whopping hangover and no aspirin. I sent him to town in the only available vehicle, our half-ton cattle truck, and Deputy Sheriff Chris Kralicek picked him up because he thought the truck was moving down the street without a driver. He couldn't see the child's head over the steering wheel. In court Chris said, "I'd like to add, Your Honor, that this young man was very polite and drives real well." Ken paid the ten-dollar fine, but he was surly about it.

Claytie frequently made Ken's life a minor hell by phoning to say, "Father, you've got to come right over here with those big brute muscles and move my piano again. I've decided to put the bar on that back wall for the party tomorrow night."

Usually he grinned sheepishly, gathered up Jake and complied—until the year one of our punier ski bums, assisting with piano moving for the first time, was buried headfirst in the snow and had to be resuscitated at the hospital.

Claytie created more uproar than a bee down a blouse front. She astonished, cheered, exasperated, and vexed us. She was a dash of cayenne pepper in a boiling pot of ragout, best in very small pinches.

We got a heavy dose of her, however, almost from the start. She moved right in with us, after a gas line leaked and blew the Aspen studio she had leased sky-high. To our first season she contributed lively background piano, hundreds of peculiar people picked up in plane and train terminals, a steady stream of drinks on the house, and great confusion when it was needed least.

Naturally the most important people in our lives were the children. And although I am not the kind to carry baby pictures in my wallet, to avoid muddy thinking I believe it is time to describe them in depth.

That first winter there were just six of them. Later, depending on my whim and/or state of health and mind, we had seven, eight, or nine. To the casual onlooker, this is apt to create confusion.

By marshaling all of my forces (I still confuse the children's ages and birthdates, while recalling that Warren G. Harding's middle name was Gamaliel), I will try to describe them The Year The Lodge Was Born.

Robin was eleven, blonde, with large brown eyes, sturdy legs, and a solemn sufferance with her role as the eldest. Sometimes she shouldered so much responsibility for her siblings that she reminded me of one of those big-eyed child amahs of the Orient. She was artistic and sensitive, with a deep domestic bent that had to be atavistic; she scorned the package mix, baked from scratch, made salad dressing with herbs I'd never met, and had already knit her first sweater. She was dear, Dutch, and motherly, while her perplexed mother was sallow, angular, and literary.

Nephew Mike at ten was an aesthete-athlete who showed signs of looking Byronic, if this is possible in a boy who is going to be seven feet tall. He was gentle and a scholar. Like Robin, he collected things, but he collected them on a warehouse scale. He collected sabers, old guns, Confederate currency, and documents on his great-grandfather, Robert Gould Shaw; also, having caught my passion for bullfighting, books on Dominguin, Ordonez, and Manolete; and, for good measure, flags, rocks, coins, trophies, knives, and manuals on the care and breeding of horses. I began writing in order to finance housing for Mike's collections, which I figured would be less work than trying to winnow anything out.

Whit was named for his maternal uncle and, I groan to report, was called Half-Whit to distinguish the two. He was nine going on the Evil Age and collected money, which he speedily spent. It was Whit who found ten-dollar bills, won turkey raffles, brought home the door prizes and befriended old ladies who remembered him in their wills. We gave up trying to guide him and simply deferred to all that good fortune. Like Alfalfa of *Little Rascals* fame, he was grinning, cowlicked, affable, and devious. His developing killer instinct indicated either Alcatraz or the U.S. Ski Team by 1972. (The U.S. team won by a hair.)

Deirdre (Dede), our niece, was now eight and she and Gwyneth (Gwendy), seven, automatically came in a pair. Gwendy was cheerful (of such sunny disposition that our guests called her DearGwen) and dark-haired Dede, dramatic and brown haired. They were presently consumed with a prim missionary zeal which had evolved out of a series of evangelistic meetings attended with a little friend. My background is sedate Episcopalian. Ken is New England Baptist, turned heathen. But we'd always believed in having the children sample synagogues, masses, and summer Bible school with a view to making their own eventual choices. At least I thought we did. When "Les Girls," their eyes as glazed as maraschino cherries, began subjecting me to selected Bible readings and announced that they were ready to "declare for the Lord," I hastily arranged after-school chores demanding their full-time attention.

Dan at three was being reared by the other children. Since they alternately spoiled and browbeat him, his personality was as unsettled as warm Jell-O. It was useless for his parents to try letting him bloom unpruned. His brothers and sisters wanted him espaliered, scrubbed pink, and mute as Marcel Marceau. Fearing him a seething mass of inner conflicts, I began referring to him as the *Enfant*

Perdu. But he remained a jaunty blend of Puck and Peck's Bad Boy. He listened to "Peter and The Wolf" while standing on his head and tumbled down the driveway on skis the size of squash rackets. His affections settled warmly over everyone, including the wicked witches in the storybooks.

As a group the children were attractive, precocious, bad, good, normal, unruly, and poised. There were days when they were depressingly average and others I thought they should be at Yale this minute. As in all large families, they knew if they quarreled anarchy would reign. They sometimes bickered. They rarely fought.

In order not to have them grow up behind our backs, we managed to isolate each child for lunch or dinner once a month. These social occasions were fraught with surprise. "Why good heavens, child, you've lost two more teeth." "You don't mean to sit there and tell us that there are *four* Scout troops in this town?" "What do you mean, you like the school because it's all white?" (That child was referring to the paint color.)

These children not only fended for each other but often for their parents. They took care of my thank you notes, family correspondence, and Christmas shopping. They lowered hems, raised movie money, sewed on buttons, cooked dinner, baked bread, fed horses, dogs and invalids, planned picnics and parties and were soon handling reservations on the telephone.

A startled Mr. Porter McPhail of Tacoma, Washington, once received full accommodation information from Daniel, then aged five. Mr. McPhail never made it to Aspen, nor did he ever recover fully from the impact of a kindergartner with the savvy of Conrad Hilton. We know. He corresponded with Daniel for years.

In all candor I can say those kids had an eventful and very offbeat childhood.

*   *   *

Uncle Whit was a weekend commuter from Denver, a six-foot-three-inch pillar of strength who covered a lot of the fronts Ken and I missed. He was unfailingly patient and loving, with that instinctual understanding of what children need for emotional sustenance. With him on hand, we had six children and three parents, and the odds were a lot more even.

Other more or less immediate members of the family were Magnë Nostdahl, Arnë Marthinsson, and Peder Klyve, who had arrived directly from the North Sea to teach skiing for Stein Eriksen, take up residence in our bunkhouse and learn English in three weeks or less. They all had apple red cheeks, bright eyes, and perplexed expressions caused by their struggles to assimilate the children's enigmatic vocabularies of "spazz," "creep," "crud," and "rat fink."

This is also as good a time as any to inventory our animals, who required almost as much time and attention as the children. In one respect we were akin to James Thurber. We acquired new dogs with disturbing regularity. People with puppies smelled us right out. Or else the children appeared in the kitchen with eyes only slightly less limpid and pleading than those of the lost creature in their arms. When it came to animals, Ken and I were never able to develop a firm stand and stay there.

By Christmas we were the owners of a boxer puppy named Damë, shipped to us by Ken's sister Barbara who was swamped in Cornell graduate school and couldn't cope with shots, feedings, and housebreaking; of our setter, Heather; of a hybrid Newfoundland, Ruffy (so consumed with an inordinate passion for Aspen Mountain that he ran to town and climbed it the moment we let him out of the lodge, thus necessitating the purchase of a lift ticket for Jake to ride to the top and retrieve him); and a magnificent Malamute, Yukon Ike of Snowplume, given to Robin by a socialite patient of Uncle Whit's who decided she preferred something smaller and in gold. There were also Claytie's Marzipan; Dan's large, wild-eyed calico cat, Marcus Aurelius; a devilish black feline named Inkwell; and a stray known as Milkbar in deference to the eleven kittens she promptly produced in our laundry room and which we were too overcome to name.

While Ken and I were cosseting our first ski guests as if they were a royal hunting party, the kids fed the animals and saw to the last-minute Christmas shopping. Back east a downtown trip had meant a chaste, chaperoned excursion to city department stores. One of Aspen's lovely fringe benefits was being able to turn the children loose without a thought for muggers, rapists, or white slavers. Ours were so thrilled at trekking from store to store without parental supervision that Jake or Ellie had to pry them off the streets almost nightly.

For our first Christmas Uncle Whit had written off ten whole days of appointments and arrived staggering under stacks of gifts, grinning owlishly through a fresh coat of snow and looking like St. Nicholas in mufti. "I'll make house calls but I won't do windows or floors," he bellowed.

With packages piled beckoningly, the lodge overflowing, and our guests happily skiing and belting down gluehwein, Ken, Jake, Uncle Whit, the children, the dogs, and I ventured into the White River National Forest a block down the road. There we waded through feathery, thigh-deep snow and cut the lodge's very own live Christmas tree, a stunning seventeen-foot blue spruce, from among millions of trees jostling each other vigorously for elbow room. Ken was disgruntled about swinging an axe in such crowded quarters. But I felt it worth every bit of time, trouble, and the one dollar we paid the U.S. Forest Service. Even their father was noticeably moved by the starry-eyed expressions of kids who'd heretofore believed that all Christmas trees sprang full-blown from super-market parking lots.

The elegant Christmas trees that decorating magazines "do" in a motif of red and white silk bows or dainty musical instruments either spring from families without children, or parents with enough money to hire an interior decorator and an armed guard. Our trees have always looked distinctly tipsy, very homegrown, heavily decorated near the bottom, and sparsely covered on top. The children, down to the babies, are unfailingly gentle with our hand-me-down ornaments, as if they were living links with their past and a kind of lifeline to the future. When we finally invited our guests to drink eggnog and help with the big Tree Trimming, I noticed our young kept the more personal antiques firmly out of reach of other, less caring hands.

On Christmas day the children were agog over new skis, boots, and parkas (furnished at cost by our friend Klaus Obermeyer, who was deeply shaken by the sheer volume of our shopping list). The highlight of the morning was blindfolding Dan while we brought his Shetland pony into the house. McDuff proved to be a mean little devil, but Dan thought he was Pegasus incarnate. All the children received their first equestrian training and suffered the hard knocks of being thrown from that surly little back.

I was once again disappointed in my number one Christmas request: a strong, motherly woman to spend her life scolding me about my dry skin and beastly hours, kneading that place in my back that knots up when I'm tired and maintaining stern Naval Academy discipline over the children's socks, my lingerie, and the kitchen cupboards. Instead I received some stylish ski and after-ski clothes that hung on me like damp wash. I'd lost so much weight that I was as scrawny as a stewing hen and every bit as sensuous.

After our own tumultuous gift exchanging, Ellie, Jake,

the children, and I labored to dispose of mountains of ribbons, wrappings, and boxes discarded in the wake of our departed ski guests. For some reason I was taken aback to find that everyone had gone skiing exactly as if this were any old day of the week.

"But it's Christmas," I protested.

"What did you expect, Martie, the Norman Luboff Choir and lodgers popping corn by the fire in their Dr. Dentons?" Ken inquired. "If people pay good money to ski, they'll ski—even on Judgment Day."

We finished the lodge work in double-quick time and Jake hollered at the mountaintops, "Ready or not, here we come." Then he, Uncle Whit, and the children bounded across the road to ski. Ellie, reduced to my tortoise pace, sank groaning into a tub of bubbles, where she wallowed half the afternoon.

By this time Ken was ski instructing for Stein, who had graciously overlooked his New England accent and lack of Nordic ancestry and put him straight to work. This left me blissfully alone with a self-basting turkey, Graham Greene, and several priceless empty hours.

Our Christmas was to be capped by a merry late-evening feast. Late, because Claytie was not only vague about mealtimes but considered eleven o'clock in the morning the first splinter of dawn. Also because our Happy Hour with guests tended to stretch into two, three, or sometimes four. We would be joined by Magnë, Arnë, and Peder, still homesick for their fjords and dazedly trying to sift through our confusing potpourri of barbaric customs.

At 8:30 that evening everyone blew in at once. Claytie arrived in fur mukluks, white beaver, raspberry Bogners, and a flurry of colorful gifts. The Norwegians gathered in clouds of aquavit fumes. And we were joined by Ulla Nillson, a tall Swede who was someone's date.

"Father!" cried Claytie to Ken. "You will be so proud of me! I have finally taken your advice and gotten myself equipped for skiing. It's been years since I've had any fresh air or exercise." (The most strenuous exercise I'd seen Claytie partake of was breakfasting in bed).

Ken, waxing all brawny, ski-instructor, down-to-brass-tacks, practical man, inquired, "What kind of boots did you buy?"

"Weeeeellll, we are going to have to wait a bit on those." Claytie's tone was suspiciously like that of a reprieved criminal. "You know my foot is bonier than a plate of trout, so I've ordered those custom-made boots from Bob Oden and David Lawrence. They made these clever plaster casts of my feet and . . ."

"Claytie, for Lord's sake why didn't you start off with something less involved and a whole lot cheaper, at least until you find out if you even like skiing?"

"Oh, pooh. You're the one who's always going on about the importance of good equipment. What's more, I have my new skis right here for your inspection. Jim Pomeroy was a dear about engraving and installing those ghastly thingamabobs."

"Bindings? Well, what kind of bindings. What kind of skis?" Ken was bristling with curiosity.

"Uuuuuum. I can't ac-tu-al-ly recall, Father. Say, haven't you children finished unwrapping your gifts yet? I need one of you to mix me a nice festive Black Russian." (At this point Claytie had promoted every child except Daniel to post-graduate bartending.) "Oh yes, the skis. Well, they're the most dreamy shade of blue, sort of a Capri cerulean. And on the toes they have that snappy-looking Olympic motif that's . . . er . . ." She had noticed the expression on Ken's face.

"Claytie," he said hollowly, "no one buys skis for their color. That's the most cockamamie thing I ever heard of."

"You know, that's just what Jim Pomeroy said, but I said that if we can color-code sheets and blankets, why not skis and ski clothes?"

"Do you mean to tell me that Jim let you talk him into

what I think are racing skis? So they'd match your parka?" Ken asked in disbelief.

"Now, Father, they're just my size, and I insisted, because they will look heavenly with all my new Bogners." (Heretofore Claytie had bought ski clothes either to worship in private or to drink in public.)

"And possibly with the complete body cast you'll be sporting after you break every bone in your back. If I'm not mistaken, and I don't believe I am, you have bought yourself Kästle Master Slaloms with the new Kofix bottoms?"

"They're yellow."

Ken groaned. "The very shade of the stripe down your back if you ever strap those things on your feet. They are very stiff and very fast, and you will not be able to survive elementary instruction in the snowplow."

The children, Jake, Ellie, and half of Scandinavia looked pityingly at Claytie, as if she'd just flunked her merit badge in boiling water. She said bleakly, "Oh, dear. I did so want you to be surprised and pleased with me."

"Never mind, love," I said. "I'm sure you can trade them in, even if they do have your name engraved on them. Isn't there something they can do about engraving?" I beseeched Ken.

"It's about as hard to remove as a tattoo," he said glumly.

Never one to admit defeat. Claytie brightened and began rapping out orders. "Mike and Whit, you boys bring those skis right in the house, they are on my car rack. Robin dear, do hurry with my Russian, and don't, please don't, overdo the Kahlua. Magnë, there's a case of Mumm's and some lovely Beaujolais in the trunk that would herniate these babies, you big men carry those. Gwendy, I believe there are a few goodies tucked in the glove compartment, do retrieve anything that looks 'gifty' and . . . . Oh my God, I forgot Mrs. Packard."

The Vikings found Mrs. Packard sitting in Claytie's Mercedes swathed in full-length wolf and a moldering buffalo that had died a violent death. She was boiled as an owl and humming happily. They bore her triumphantly into the house.

"I was playing the piano at the Jerome," Claytie exclaimed delightedly, "and would you believe she has a suite there for the winter and levitates people right in their living rooms?" Mrs. Packard sat in our wing chair, still humming and oblivious to her surroundings.

"She doesn't look as if she could lift herself out of that seat," Ken said darkly. "In fact, she looks as settled as Whistler's mother."

"Isn't she cute?" trilled Claytie, as pleased as if she'd found sunken treasure.

Mrs. Packard was not cute. She was a slightly bawdy old lady very pickled on the hoof. After a few cosmetic tuckups, we later learned, she had given up and let her dewlaps drop for good. As Ken said, "You couldn't lift that face with a two-ton truck."

"When does she levitate?" I asked nervously.

"Well, the confluences of the planets aren't right at the moment," Claytie said. (Either her trimesters were out of sync, or the Arcturians were on the rampage, or the planets were overheated, we found out later. It was always something.) "But her hour will come," Claytie assured us solemnly. "Now, Martha Jane, I believe you and I are the same height. Don't just sit there, Ducks, stand up!" Claytie began circling, fixing me with the penetrating gaze of a Mother Superior.

Claytie was back in charge. This was going to be *her* Merry Christmas. She had given all of the children musical instruments, and soon there were pained but happy bleatings, hootings, and drumbeats from their quarters. The Norwegians switched from aquavit to champagne without pausing to draw breath, and shortly were bleating and hooting happily too. I found myself the dazed new owner of cerulean blue Kästle Master Slaloms. And Jake, Ellie, and Ken all blinked quizzically at wildly implausible gifts along the lines of mink-handled corkscrews.

After dinner we sang carols in three languages, Mrs. Packard thrumming contentedly off tune in the background. As Ken and I raised enfeebled voices in song, we looked at each other, at the silent trees stretching snow-covered arms about our windows in benediction, at my brother and our offspring glowing with holiday joy, and at our wonderfully wacky new friends. We weren't one bit sorry that we'd gone ahead and done it.

CHAPTER 7

But Is Your Life Your Own?

WHAT WE had done, we knew, was more than throw up a building, mail out a lot of half-truths and open our doors for business. An old-fashioned ski lodge circa the fifties and sixties was the sum of many intangibles: shining copper, dancing firelight, charming people, a forever-festive air. A ski lodge either made shimmering vacation visions come true, or you had just another dreary boarding house on your hands.

Right from the start we tried to show our guests that we cared. (Ken even accused me of tying them to my umbilical cord.) There were months when I waded through so many personal crises that I felt like a cross between a visiting nurse and the poor man's Ann Landers.

Our first paying customers were paragons of charm and forebearance who overlooked the "raw" in our "beginnings" with determined good will. Em O'Berry was a delightful lady engineer who arrived with her just-as-delightful Stanford-student daughter Terry. Marilyn and Ray Ellen, from El Dorado, Arkansas, became new friends who returned many times, bringing their town behind them. Ditto urbane bachelors Sid Black and Bill Reader of Los Angeles. Nancy and Ross Grimes and their three children from Evergreen, Colorado, would eventually put in enough time with us to claim de facto family membership. Naz Mardikian, whose husband owned the Omar Khayyam Restaurant in San Francisco, was the first Armenian we'd ever met. She endeared herself to all by coolly smothering a blazing log on the lounge carpet with her sable coat.

Our first season capacity was thirty-four guests, give or take a few, and our first houseful all blue ribbon winners.

Our guest lounge was our special pride. Its leviathan fireplace rose to a high, beamed ceiling. Sloping glass window walls framed a breathtaking panorama outside. In Aspen's thin, dry air colors were always high, even in winter. One grew breathless from the intensity of space, at sight of that indescribable sky. In the distance, Maroon Bells and Pyramid Peak, snow-capped all year, rose like ageless lamaseries piercing the heavens. At their feet, giant Douglas firs, blue spruce, lodgepole, and ponderosa pines marched in gradations of green down the valley, across our Lower Forty, and along Maroon Creek's banks below.

Beneath the skirts, around the feet, and on every side of our great evergreens clambered young, playful choke-cherries, scrub oak, serviceberry bushes, and adolescent aspens. Even in wintertime undress, these youngsters provided graceful footnotes of snow-laden branches. Here and there one could glimpse the gala scarlet of rose hips, the yellow of Oregon grape, and bright-berried elder.

Led by choruses of pine siskins busy about their house-keeping, a cast of birds performed daily matinees in marvelous color and sound. No tropical aviary ever outdazzled our collection of downy woodpeckers; red-banded flickers; or plump nuthatches and chickadees, their black and brown furry caps pulled over their eyes. Flocks of rose-breasted grosbeaks and yellow, black, and white cedar waxwings vied chattily for seating space. Ruby-crowned kinglets and gaudy jays were drawn to our theater by berries, bark, cones, grubs, and the children's plump suet desserts. Down in the creek, water ouzels darted. Often a snowy owl eyed us in sleepy midday disdain. Hawks and a golden eagle swept down from the mountainsides. Or a ptarmigan, that most foolish of birds, tried to bumble his way indoors for a chat.

Against this stunning slice of cyclorama, our lounge decor of leather, slate, and sheepskin was liberally laced with antiques, paintings, books, and good will. Tucked in the peak of the A-frame above our front entrance was the Crow's Nest, a delectable children's hideaway reached by a tree house-style ladder.

We were undoubtedly too cluttered for *Architectural Digest*, but the overall effect was one of warmth and welcome. Here we would spend many wonderful hours with legions of fascinating people who were to become lifelong friends. (Although, as Rose had warned, there would be times we had cause to regret our little leitmotiv, "Every guest a member of the family.")

An added attraction that we'd ballyhooed ringingly in our brochures was the après-ski hour. Taking our cue from Ria, we'd contracted for a minimum of one get-acquainted cocktail party per week plus daily gluehwein and hors d'oeuvres—to say nothing of ski movie nights, holiday celebrations, and observances of anniversaries, birthdays, and nonstop ski runs. All of this may sound a mere bagatelle. But the gluehwein alone meant sentencing each of us to the equivalent of high tea every last day of our lives at four o'clock sharp. Many an afternoon would come when we were sick to death of this commitment. But each week brought a crop of new guests simply salivating for the good talk and free wine and edibles heralded in those damned brochures.

Gluehwein, a classic German hot drink, exudes a heady, spicy odor that's inordinately appealing to bone-chilled skiers. But I'd like to add that after years of cooking and ladling out the stuff, those highly touted spices are enough to make a seasoned sailor puke. With a barely concealed curl of the lip, Ken and I, over the years, have turned down hundreds of invitations to hot wine parties. We consider them in a class with picnicking at a penitentiary.

Well, I was just stirring in the last of the cinnamon for our first after-Christmas gluehwein in our vaunted perfect setting for love and laughter when I suddenly paused and said to Ken, "Say, what will happen if we do get a spazz in the lodge? We've been spoiled, you know, by fun-loving nuts who don't give a hoot about rough edges."

Ken, ducking out of his ski school sweater, said blankly, "A what in the lodge?"

"A spazz. Current child vernacular for 'creep'," I said musingly. "I suppose we can't expect every guest to be bright, witty, well-mannered, tolerant, and a joy forever."

"I don't know why not," Ken said with maddening male placidity.

"Why is it that men can never understand the disastrous effects of just one big bore?" I sighed. "A bigot or a bigmouth is all it takes to ruin a dinner or a ski week." The mere thought of being trapped in our own building, maybe for days, with a paying customer of this ilk made me shudder over the wine kettle. Then I thrust the qualm aside in the faint, faraway hope that it might happen much later or never at all.

It happened almost immediately.

The Witless group had contacted us early in October about Christmas reservations for two couples with one child each. They wanted, they said, to reserve one of our four-person bunkrooms and add cots. They lived deep in the heart of Texas but "not deep enough to tap any awl wells, har, har," Mr. Witless had roared. They needed to economize, he explained.

Since none of our rooms were finished or furnished at the time, it was difficult for me to visualize space. But those bunkrooms were very small and had been designed for four college students (so long as they weren't basketball players) or four children (preferably underweight and prepubescent) or in a pinch for any four freeloaders we wished to dissuade from lengthy visits. Protesting feebly, I even went so far as to mail off the exact room dimensions, drawn to scale on a tidy little floor plan.

I just knew that that space would not hold six people unless they cared to curl up like cling peaches in a jar. I said so. Unfortunately I was too green to raise an objection and then sustain it.

"Thayat's all right, doll," insisted Mr. Witless silkily on the phone, "we all dohn need nothin' fancy. You juss save us thayat l'il old room." The man exuded the oily bonhomie of Jimmy "the Weasel" Fratiano.

After more phone calls, special deliveries, and wires from somewhere along the Rio Grande (all costing far more than I felt the Witlesses could afford in their meager circumstances), they finally convinced me that they truly did not care about the size of their space; that they didn't plan to be in their room except to sleep, shower, and change; and that they were looking forward to being regular "lounge lizards" in our beautiful lodge. With misgivings, I booked them.

The Witlesses arrived late on the afternoon of December twenty-sixth, directly on the heels of six thousand other skiers who'd reserved every accommodation in Aspen up to and including the empty attics and pigeon lofts. After a nervous welcoming speech, I registered them, a formality I often overlooked in the heat of arrival, and escorted them to the lounge. There I ran through the litany of breakfast, Happy Hour, and scheduled holiday parties. Then I showed them to their quarters and the very first thing Mr. Witless said was, "Mah Gawd, we cain't fit in this yere pipsqueak room. Show us youah biggah ones, honey."

I'll admit I wasn't at my most eloquent. "You're kidding," I gasped.

He stared at me with the stony eyes of a water snake. "Youah the one 'at's playin' jokes, sistah, not me."

I was dead serious, at the end of a pretty frayed rope, and I detest being called "sister."

"Mr. Witless, I explained to you that Christmas is prime time. I described these accommodations to a tee. And I told you that everything from here to Salt Lake City would be booked. I don't believe you paid attention to a word I said."

"Check the puhfect hostess," drawled his wife, a large, rough-spoken slattern with doorknob hair, a parrot mouth, and knockers bursting out of her soiled décolletage. The other couple, then and later, were shifty-eyed and uncommunicative.

Shaking with fatigue and fury, I seethed at Witless *père*. "You had every chance to make a choice earlier. I begged you to take larger quarters. Well, it's too late now. There aren't any bigger rooms, *or any rooms at all*, not between here and Donner Pass." It was a struggle for me to speak firmly with my knees playing a noisy descant below. The mildest difference of opinion over a gin game reduces me to mush.

"You didn't make things vereh cleah," snarled Mrs. Witless in her bourbon baritone. "We suhtinly woulda prefuhed stayin' back in Tayexus to sharin' this mizzuble cubbeh hole."

Oh, why didn't you? I moaned inwardly and stalked off to the office for the carbon copies of the voluminous Witless/Sterling correspondence, by now thick enough for publication. It was a futile gesture. Embittered lodge owners had warned me, "Don't bother to drag out your correspondence. A problem guest will only refuse to read a line of it." Sure enough. With a wave of a tarantula hand, Witless *père* dismissed those hundreds of carefully chosen words, including his own, as so much hogwash.

Later when I described their actions to Ria, she said with a scowl that the Witlesses were undoubtedly pulling one of the nastier stunts in the hotel business: arrive, raise a terrible stink, and embarrass the luckless proprietor into plusher rooms or treatment at rock bottom prices. In a way, the Witlesses finally pulled it off.

Miserable craven that I am, I located big bluff Iglook, shoved him into the fray and fled to the kitchen to replenish the cheese trays and my resolve. If Ken didn't exactly establish loving rapport with the Witlesses, he at least convinced them that we'd better all make the best of a bad situation. They settled in with a lot of dirty looks, even dirtier language, one case of branch water and one of bourbon (no doubt an economy measure to save on food costs), and sent their two whey-faced children to the lounge with orders to "Stay theah."

Well, I decided miserably, Christmas comes but once a year. And I'll just bet those poor Witless kids got nothing but knuckle sandwiches in their stockings.

Gathering up cheese trays and cocktail napkins, I added some popcorn balls and headed for the lounge to spread cheer among the young.

"Hi there," I said brightly to the Witless boy, who was about eight and somehow hanging by his knees from a ceiling beam. "What's your name?" I asked in what the children call my "sincere" voice.

"Nyaaaaah," he answered, sticking out his tongue and adding a short and unattractive word.

Uh oh, a chip off the old crock, I decided bitterly. The kid's upbringing had obviously been Early Inquisition. I tried the partnership approach. "How would you like to help me string some more lights on top of that tall tree? It looks a bit bare and—"

"Nyaaaaah," he repeated, sticking his tongue out to where I could have lopped it off with the fireplace poker. I contemplated it.

One more college try, I decided grimly. "Say, we have a whole posse of children here, some of them about your age, and—"

He interrupted by dropping lice-like from the beam and uttering a really vile word. ". . . and they're all bigger than you and either you shape up, kiddo, or they'll be happy to cut you down to size." There went Krafft-Ebing and Spock down the behavioral drain. But then I never have put up with conduct from strange kids that I wouldn't countenance in my own.

Undaunted, the Witless monkey darted to the fireplace and hurled a string of sausage-like objects onto the blazing logs. There was an interval while we waited for the last firecracker to explode.

"Okay, Guy Fawkes," I barked, clutching him by his dirty shirt, "I want your name, age, and serial number. On the double."

Trapped in my steely grip, he stuttered, "M—my name h'ain't G—guy-what's-it. H'it's J—Joel."

"Been running live ammunition in from Mexico, Joel boy?"

"W—wahl, y—yeah. But evrabody does h'it daown home." He was no longer cheekier than a vacuum cleaner salesman, undoubtedly because I looked menacing and he was out of fireworks. In fact he was so close to tears that I decided it wasn't my job to imbue the child with raison d'être, just reform him to a point where he wouldn't maim or unnerve any of our nicer guests.

"Got any more cherry bombs on you?" I asked in low, threatening tones.

"D—downsteahs in the s—suitcases," he confessed with a frightened howl as I tightened my grip.

"All right, friend, you're cooked. You and your explosives. We're going to confiscate them, understand?" He nodded shakily. I paused and underlined each word carefully. "Tonight we are having a party for our guests. We will count on you to behave like a gentleman. And to help. And without another word of that gutter language. Hear?"

There was a giggle from his girl friend, a wizened child of perhaps seven whom I'd been too nettled to notice. "I," she announced gleefully, "wet the bed."

"Dear heaven," I groaned, "you two had better come downstairs with me."

When our children returned from skiing, they took over with a minimum of blistering comment. "Those two sure are from hunger," Robin whispered distastefully.

Gwendy said, "Boy, do they have rotten manners."

Whit asked, "If he hits me again should I hit him back or try to reason with him?"

"Use good judgment and no fisticuffs, gang." And I left the Capables in charge.

In a few hours a reconstructed twosome were partially tamed and happy as mudlarks. And we needn't have worried about their elders infiltrating the cheery climate of our guest lounge. They remained in that "mizzuble cubbeh hole" undoubtedly plotting to stop up the plumbing and burn all our blankets. By evening they were well-fueled with Jim Beam and had throttled up to a high-pitched whickering that did not invite interruption. Joel and his wettish friend, apparently abandoned, stayed with us through après-ski gluehwein, buffet supper, and the last solemn chorus of "Old Folks At Home," by which time Joel was asleep with his thumb in his ear and his head in Robin's lap.

I just hated having to send them off to bed amid the catcalls, shrieking laughter, and ringing epithets with which their families were recalling "Silent Night, Holy Night." But we decided that if we tucked them in with our brood there was the off chance they would be missed, probably between four and six o'clock in the morning.

The following morning Witless *mère* staggered in to lounge breakfast in a tatty crepe de chine wrapper that barely contained her bobbling boobs, her Medusa coiffure in dirty plastic hair curlers, and brayed that her husband needed coffee but we could bet our sweet asses *she* wasn't carrying any down to the damn drunk. Ken and I looked at each other and both felt that this ordeal might prove longer than a summer in Chihuahua.

As Ken readied himself for the ski mountain, he said through tight lips, "We have to get that old harlot out of here before she turns up naked to the crotch and has her way with those college boys on the sideboard."

"I'll do my darnedest," I promised.

I squandered a precious part of the day calling every large motel in and around town in the wild gamble that someone might have canceled, broken a leg, or died. Late in the afternoon I hit George Madsen and the jackpot. The Madsens had just built a two-apartment chalet and had, oh joy, an empty one.

I explained our predicament and said, "We'll be happy to pay the difference in rent ourselves, George." (Our Pyrrhic victory cost us dearly.) "But I have to be honest, they're a bad bunch."

"They won't bother a soul over here, and we're happy to fill the space. Can you imagine our people backing out on Christmas night?"

"No, but I'll pray for them." Then I added, "Keep an eye on your blankets. Merry Christmas and God bless."

It wasn't difficult to satisfy the Witless group that they would be deliriously happy in the lovely two-room Madsen chalet for exactly the same cheap rent they were paying in our crummy bunkroom. They moved out in a stampede of baggage, bourbon, and howling, protesting children. "But ah wanna stay heah," wept Joel, and I was all set to go to court for custody. "Given time, we could have done something for those children," I said heatedly to Ken.

Ken belonged to the school of thought that interfering with guests' personal lives was on a par with interrupting childbirth. "Martie," he pointed out for the first of what would be a thousand times, "this is a ski lodge we're operating, not a halfway house."

George Madsen was the editor of the *Aspen Flyer* and told us later he had it on the best authority through news channels that the Witless crowd was suspected of bootlegging stolen army goods over several state lines. We could believe it.

It's evident that you're better off halting the shady element at your perimeter defenses. Most innkeepers develop a kind of sixth sense about potential troublemakers. Friends in the business assured us that they could spot, even smell, a check bouncer or blanket thief for blocks. Fortunately we rarely harbored either. But only, I always felt, because crooks got our number first—as an intimate, fraternal little gathering where they would be remembered until their dying day. It's a good thing, too. I am the sort who would welcome good old "Legs" Diamond and that sweet "Greasy Thumb" Gulik because they both dressed impeccably and had soulful Sicilian eyes.

We immediately filled the vacated bunkroom with four precious girls from the University of Wisconsin who were weepingly grateful for not having to camp out in their chilly Volkswagon. Then we recounted our blessings and went back to celebrating the holidays.

Not content with a mere Merry Christmas and our triumph over the Witlesses, I decided (amid loud moans from a weary household) that we should personally see to everyone's Happy New Year.

"If people wanted a damned social director, they could have taken a cruise," Ken said heatedly to the empty air.

I informed him that we had to finish our first year with a flourish, in honor of those valiant pioneers who had come ahead and taken a chance on us. "It's the very least we can do," I assured old doubting Thomas.

And thus we discovered just how unique our house-party hospitality really was.

New Year's Eve was not long under way before we divined that we were the only lodge in Aspen throwing a party. A whole lot of skiers had already divined the very same thing. By eleven o'clock there were so many strangers in the place that we resembled O'Hare Airport at rush hour, and so much noise we nearly broke the sound barrier. By eleven thirty Ken was hopelessly lost in the crush, and I knew I wouldn't see him until sometime next year. By midnight hordes of exuberant partyers were jammed in our lounge, waiting in line outside, eating our ham, turkey, and aspic molds, and liberally helping themselves to our guests' liquor stocks.

Backed against a wall and facing the mottled specter of schizophrenia, I made a last-ditch effort and hurtled across the room to greet a group of attractive younger men who had just stormed the entrance. "Happy New Year!" I shrieked gaily as I proffered my hand. "I'm Martie Sterling and I . . ."

One of the young men picked up and then discarded the hand with a faint sneer of distaste. (I am not the type tall dark strangers invite to Rio for Carnival. I am the type they sell fake artifacts to.) Another remarked haughtily over my head, "Great party, wonder who's throwing it."

It was then I realized just how much had slipped out of my grasp and that, one way or another, I had better get organized.

CHAPTER 8

Who Ever Heard of Norma Shearer?

WELL, MY LACK OF organization was certainly appalling and our location supposedly wanting. But our beginnings had been encouraging. It seemed we had plenty to offer after all, we decided a little smugly.

We had: our well-known open door policy; that spectacular view of Pyramid Peak and the Maroon Bells; a very busy game trail visible from our lounge, where bull elk pridefully escorted harems of cows; coyotes, families of deer, badgers, and wildcats traversing the backside of Buttermilk Mountain on their way to water; Maroon Creek tumbling musically and picturesquely below; a highly attractive lodge life; a ski mountain in our laps; and—we had Stein.

Stein Eriksen was the first, possibly the greatest, of the all-time legendary skiing greats—a blazing blue-eyed, swivel-hipping, six-foot Norwegian who emerged from the post-World War II Winter Olympics wreathed in medals and dimpled smiles. Now, some five years after his sweep of the World Ski Championships, here Stein was, the director of the brand new Highlands Ski School right at our front door.

I was so disoriented that first year that my most breathless leisure pursuit was watching Norma Shearer float down the staircase of the Jerome Hotel in clouds of chiffon, followed at a worshipful distance by her ski instructor husband Marty Arrougé, and gazed at adoringly by me. We who are climacteric will go to the grave remembering Norma as Marie Antoinette en route to the guillotine, every shining hair in place, sculpted head riding majestically above the clattering tumbrel, eyes luminous with belladonna. She was more queenly than Mary Queen of Scots, and it was only proper the world should be at her feet. Unless you count Iglook, who spent an unedifying childhood following Hoot Gibson in Saturday afternoon cliff hangers. His inevitable, scornful rejoinder: "Who ever heard of Norma Shearer?"

Well, I'd never heard of Stein Eriksen. Guests' initial references to the man found me with my mind on bedding and bath mats, too preoccupied to care about the chimeric ski world beyond my immediate domain. Between Thanksgiving and Christmas I'd done everything for that lodge short of weaving the carpets; and even over the holidays I never set a ski boot on those beckoning, snowy slopes.

The children, however, were under no such constraints. They'd been skiing since the first faint trickle of snow. At their ages they were not much help around a hotel (their day would come), so they toddled right on over to the Highlands to get acquainted. Since the start of the season they had spent every waking, nonschool daylight hour meeting that mountain and the people skiing it.

Because there were six of them, and only two of us, I frequently lost touch. But I did hold scattered attendance checks, and one Sunday afternoon I scolded the entire posse for missing lunch. "You can't ski without recharging your batteries," I protested.

"It's okay, Mom," Whit said airily. "Stein bought us lunch and I had two hotdogs." Then they all ran off to wax their skis, dragging Danny behind them.

I felt certain that the only person who'd possibly buy

lunch for six ravenous children must be a very dirty old man, and I yelled frantically, "Stein who?"

"Oh, you know, Stein!" echoed down the hallway.

I didn't know then, but I did before long, and a whole lot more than I cared to. Fawning, swooning females (nowadays known as groupies) began spilling over onto our doorstep. Writers wrote wistfully, "Please God, just once like Stein." Folksingers composed paeans to his symphonic grace. Whole families arrived, rushed to our office, and asked eagerly, "Where do we see Stein?"

Slowly it dawned on me that Stein was more than the nebulous Norwegian for whom Ken Sterling casually taught skiing. He was a world-class celebrity with a face as recognizable as Dwight D. Eisenhower's and a whole lot prettier, who was besieged by autograph hounds, and who attracted great big crowds of panting, paying customers.

Stein was a very handy legend to have on hand, a living advertisement for fresh air and Viking blood. His noble profile and golden locks were attributable to good genes, his rippling muscles to Spartan training, his lack of tooth plaque to aquavit.

Furthermore, he was reinforced by baskets of medals and trophies that, melted down for scrap, would have armed a regiment. He also had a flair for merchandising that, twenty-five years later, still keeps him on magazine covers and sweater labels, in ski movies and Chap-stick ads and spearheading elegant new resorts.

On skis the man was a cross between Super Spider and a descending angel.

If skiers missed Stein on weekdays they could see him any Sunday at high noon, when he did his famous flip. With the élan of a Flying Wallenda, he would give a pat to a vicious-looking jump hill, sidestep to the top, pause dramatically, wave jauntily to the crowd and at length roar down the course, hit the jump, stretch into a Swan, turn over in midair and land to thunderous applause. (Go ahead, titter, all you freestylers and hotdoggers out there. Just keep in mind that Stein was the first and, back then, the only. What's more, he performed his acrobatics on skis the size of boxcars.)

I know this stretches credulity, but a few decades ago there were not thousands of speed-skiing, death-defying, gung ho American kids vying in grueling instructors' clinics for the dubious distinction of braving glacial air to teach skiing to athletic defectives. There was in fact such a dearth of good instructors that Stein had to import instructors in shipments, like his reindeer sweaters.

It was thus that a veritable Third Wave of Norsemen—farmboys and sailors from Norway, gymnasts from Denmark, sheepherders from Iceland—hit the New World. To our children the names of these Northern lights—Ulfarr, Magnë, Steinthør, Finn-Eddy, Arnë, Peder—all ornately garnished with umlauts and virgules, were at first so unintelligible and their origins so confusing that they simply lumped them together as the Vikings.

When Magnë Nostdahl, Arnë Marthinsson, and Peder Klyve climbed off the boat, they could scarcely speak English. We believe they got across the country by grinning and pointing. By the time they appeared at our door, they were shocked within an inch of their young lives. They'd fully expected gold in the streets. All they found was the same old snow. It was an added blow for them to discover that if they didn't teach they wouldn't eat. There were few guaranteed ski school salaries in those days and, particularly in the lean months of January and March, an instructor had to hustle like a Harlem pool shark to make the most meager living. Hustling in Norwegian is about as productive as pimping in Shaker Heights, and until the Vikings could improve their English, they lived on ski cafeteria leftovers, our venison stew, and the Red Onion Restaurant Special, which cost $1.50 and fortunately fed a lumberjack. For months Magnë and Arnë ordered one Special per sitting, each of them alternating meat and salad one night, bread and vegetables the next.

Later in the season Magnë, who was fortuitously dark-complexioned, obtained a night job as a Chinese waiter at Trader Ed's Restaurant. Ed himself was fighting off foreclosure by operating his entire restaurant on an extension cord plugged into an absentee owner's apartment upstairs. The place was consequently as dark as a tomb (and nearly as dank), and unsuspecting tourists, who couldn't be expected to detect the difference between a Kowloon and a Bergen accent, never noticed Magnë's European bone structure.

Our children never picked up much Norwegian (nobody picks up Norwegian except other Norwegians), but they did spend some of their formative years trying to teach Magnë and Arnë English.

The Vikings had accents as heady as *røget sild*, with a rocking chair lilt that always made me a little queasy. To compound their problems, and ours, some of them spoke Landsmaal from the old Norse and others Riksmaal from the Danish, and often could barely understand each other.

Since the Vikings not only needed to master basic English, but also advanced Reverse Shoulder terminology for Stein's ski classes, the children held regular speech clinics in our kitchen.

"Listen, Arney, you're not supposed to say 'a lot of nail.' It's 'nails,' plural."

"Gosh, Magnë, why are you such a spazz about an old J? It's not pee-yam-mahs, it's pah-jam-mahs, for Pete's sake."

"Who izz dis Pete?"

"Oh, for crying out loud."

The children taught the Vikings such useful Americanisms as how to burp at will, calling a toilet a "can," and a failure either a "moron," "spazz," "dope," or "creep"; the use of homilies on the order of "holy macaroni," which came out as "holy barcarolli," and "for cripe's sake"; and how to play and win at stud poker and seven-card-draw.

Despite these inauspicious beginnings, the Vikings

married local girls, became citizens, successful business-men, fathers of families. Ken and I are crazy about them, even when they consume that form of hemlock known as aquavit that makes a man babble like a baboon.

Magnë, Peder, and Arnë were only the beginning in an army of young aliens who stormed our doors, and even-tually we harbored more immigrants than Ellis Island.

In time I grew accustomed to having Stein in our laps, bunny types sprawled around our lounge, Vikings in our beds, and celebrities all over the place. Not that we turned into a Playboy Mansion West. Again it was just that old-fashioned hospitality that Mother used to serve.

Neither Iglook nor I ever learned to play the zither or yodel. But boy, did we acquire a reputation for a decent dry martini. We did not throw parties just to flex our so-cial muscles, but somehow they kept on happening. (Ken always claimed we were personally responsible for the six-ties expression, "a happening.") Following that first New Year's Eve debacle, our renown as Perle Mestas became so entrenched that we never fully overcame it. It was fur-ther reinforced by fun-loving skiers who heard about us as far away as Atlanta, arrived and threw parties of their own. Lodge owners all over town checked in guests and said, "As soon as you're unpacked, go right on out to the Heatherbed, they're having a party." They knew they could count on us five nights out of seven.

It was thus, over the years, that we attracted crowds the size of Coxey's Army. And thus that I strolled into my own sauna to find Art Linkletter, Teddy Kennedy, and Jane Powell draped in our towels and purifying their pores with our steam (they were not our guests and none of us had been formally introduced). And that I looked up from the canapés into the violet eyes of Kim Novak or the famous orbs of Hugh O'Brien, Lance Reventlow, Jill St. John, and Lana Turner. It's an added attraction to have celebrities around a hotel, and they were sweet about sending long-stemmed roses by the dozen. But how I used to wish that more of them were paying us room and board.

Aspen's early appeal for the world-traveled was, in part, its inaccessibility. Flying Cessna 310s, Bert Simons of the young and brazen Aspen Airways was bringing in maybe thirty passengers a day and didn't count for much in the transportation sweepstakes. Most of our skiers faced a dismal Hobson's choice. They could drive a car over the top of the Rockies, braving blizzards, blowouts, and snowslides. Or they could catch the grand old D.&R.G. railroad to Glenwood Springs; arrive at midnight (all luggage lost); climb into rickety, very draughty buses for the forty mile ride to Aspen, be dumped unceremoniously at a dingy downtown bus depot (all luggage lost); and at one o'clock in the morning, having already encountered every stage in Dante's *Inferno*, be met by a fleet of idling, smoke-blowing station wagons and weary, short-fused drivers who bellowed, "Blue Spruce, Blue Spruce over here," "Hillside, Hillside," "Anyone for the Heatherbed?" Lodge owners lost a lot of sleep. And arriving skiers lost sleep, perspective, heart, and most of their luggage.

The train/stage trip goes a long way toward explaining how so many innocent, unsuspecting flatlanders chose to drive themselves in the depth of winter into the labyrinth of the Colorado Rockies. And why, once here, people were inclined to hole up and stay.

When writer Leon Uris knocked at our door one stormy, late December evening that first year, he was waxen-faced, his voice a hoarse croak. Lee was an ex-Marine who'd spent the war years crawling around a lot of Pacific atolls under fire. But he was also a Baltimore boy who'd never in his life encountered an eleven-thousand-foot mountain pass in a driving storm with snow hurling itself head-on like millions of darts at a dartboard. Our treatment by this time was standard. We thrust a strong drink into his lifeless hands.

Lee lived to overcome acrophobia and snow blindness and fall in love with Aspen. Eventually he signed on forever, and instead of commuting from Encino to the mountains he began building his own Red Mountain home and commuting between there and his Heatherbed office. He spent a year with us writing *Armageddon* and splitting our firewood. Since then Lee has progressed through five more best-selling novels and from scatter-shot ski beginnings to the Deluxe Bomber Model skier.

Life in the high country is not life at the Algonquin Round Table. But writers seemed to find us out. I was transported when they did. Elaine and Kenneth Tynan arrived with their typewriters, and so did Alex Haley, and I delighted in making our guests tiptoe around in the manner of industrial spies any time I thought someone's muse was ticking.

Unhappily all was not roses, name dropping, and advance reservations. We were about to discover that Aspen had more skiers than it could accommodate only twice a year—over the Christmas holidays and during the last two weeks in February. The rest of the time we were on threadbare knees begging people to find us; concocting low-season, dirt-cheap package plans; creating Winterskol as an added January attraction; and contriving dozens of crowd-pleasing gimmicks to lure the world's still puny ski populace away from St. Moritz and Sun Valley.

We were not very successful, and there would be entire weeks when I felt like a Tupperware lady with only two people at her party.

CHAPTER 9

The Pause That Assesses

SUDDENLY on the fifth of January we had waved our last paying skier off to Omaha and come to in a lodge as still as the grave and nearly as empty—unless we counted the children, Ellie, Jake, Claytie, the Vikings, and the largest indebtedness this side of Washington, D.C. This was our first furtive glimpse into that dark crater labeled "Deficit," and I can tell you that it was a bigger shock than Krakatoa.

When I realized that the *Sturm und Dräng* was done, that I was indeed all alone by the telephone, I crept disconsolately into an old car coat and across town to shed despair over Ria's broad shoulders. It didn't help to find the Vagabond completely booked, with a comfortable quota of two people for every room.

"Ria, where have I gone wrong?" I wailed. "Over Christmas, we were turning away reservations like Chicago during a convention. Now we might as well have a communicable disease."

Ria poured scalding cups of coffee, cut into some of her fresh küchen, slipped out of her Capezios and said, "Martie, we've had this lodge for six years and this is the first season we've been filled for January. It doesn't happen overnight."

"But why?"

"Oh, dozens of reasons. People are broke after the holidays. Businesses must inventory. Income taxes lie dead ahead. January you have to sell."

"I don't know why we worried a minute over January thaws," I said bitterly. "There aren't enough customers to care."

"I know, I know," Ria said soothingly. "It just doesn't seem right. There are no lift lines. The snow's like seven-minute frosting. No one has to fight for a restaurant table."

"And, as an extra added attraction, the Sterlings can be seen standing in line for the public dole."

"You know you can always borrow money from Bill and me to tide you over." Ria was that kind of a friend from the start.

"Sure, I can always take in washing, too." My voice crackled like a shortwave receiver at the thought of that final solution.

"You're going to make it, Martie. You have a charming, very personal lodge. People will discover this through time, friendships, word of mouth. Your guests will have fun, come back and bring or send everyone they know. Meanwhile, you wait. And if you know what's good for you, you'll relax and regroup while you have the chance. This business ages a woman fast."

"Oh, I don't know. I don't feel any older, say, than the Battle of Bull Run."

Heeding Ria's sage advice, I dragged myself wearily back to the "slough of despond" and keeled over on a pile of pillows in front of the fire.

During the next few days, as I regained strength, balance, and two pounds, Ken and I assessed our disorderly debut in the lodge business.

Well, we'd certainly learned a thing or two. The first lesson regarded our privacy. There was none, not ever anymore. A ski lodge owner has less time to himself than a fraternity housemother with sixty boys on her palsied hands.

I now knew what it was to sit up all night with a case of muscle pull or stomach flu, then appear disheveled over the breakfast muffins to make sure those three new guests had been introduced to everyone. There would be times, and more than a few, when I was so unfocused that I'm sure our women guests suspected me of morning tippling. (Men guests were too chivalrous to entertain such thoughts.)

Then, just when we thought everyone was off to the mountain, the work under control—well, under way—and I'd slumped into a chair sighing, "Peace at last," all hell would break loose in the guise of eight college boys who burst in from Duluth with greetings from someone's cousin, and I would feel obliged to make dozens of phone calls to find them (cheap) beds (always over Christmas); or three couples from Des Moines who dropped by to be shown "all over this lovely lodge"; or a call from the hospital saying one of our guests had been brought in, and her husband was skiing another mountain or possibly in a foreign country, and would I pile into a parka and get over there to assuage her hysteria?

The pleasant little "one minute to ourselves" had become a wraithlike thing of the past.

Well, we'd survived the first onslaught, and we were certain we wanted it this way. After all, we could have elected to operate a thirty-six-unit motel with fast, impersonal service at a busy highway juncture. It would have been more profitable. A lot less wearing. And hardly any fun at all.

Pace and partnership, we'd found, were vital. Although we loved meeting and knowing and catering to people, we were already learning to conserve powder and shot, and that we'd better proceed hand in hand. We'd met a number of bibulous lodge husbands who skied with guests all day and drank with them half the night, who threw wide the front door, hollered, "Come on in, everybody," and tapped a fresh case of liquor weekly. I had also noted that their wives were invariably dun-colored and in need of prompt hospitalization. A Mom-and-Pop ski lodge was a full-time job for mom *and* pop, and it required a high degree of sobriety, dedication, and teamwork from both partners.

The grimmest aspect of my part in the partnership all fell under the heading of "Office." I wouldn't exactly refer to the place as a hellhole, but in the office lurked those account books, telephone directories, sales tax files, IRS forms, reservation letters, and other printed matter designed to make the reluctant businesswoman tremble like a fig leaf.

New math, old math, any math has always been dispiriting to me. My checkbooks resemble the Rosetta Stone. I will go to my grave never having known algebra. I am a woman who loves libraries, yet the Dewey Decimal System defeats me. My imprecision with numbers drives Ken to shingles. When I recall a story about our "thousands" of Pennsylvania friends, he interrupts with "Less than one hundred, Martie." Or when I am describing the hundreds of fish we caught down the coast of Ensenada, he'll say, "We caught twenty-three that day."

The point is, my kind of imprecision turned loose on a business could totter the House of Usher. A woman who casually substitutes hundreds and thousands for tens and twenties is simply never going to make her CPA happy.

Gradually I came up with some personalized solutions that worked well. One of these was having guests tote up their own bills. After watching my struggles with simple addition, the guests were visibly relieved. They enjoyed the responsibility, and I was off the hook. If there were errors, I'm sure they were in our favor.

In addition to my broad general duties in promotion, correspondence, and bookkeeping, I was also chief factotum and head housekeeper. These jobs were more my speed, as I believed I was a washerwoman in my last incarnation. Ken and Jake made a bed so taut you could have glissaded on their sheets. But I rather liked listening to Ellie's bogtrotter gab as we scrubbed bathrooms and caused mirrors to glisten. By January we had used enough Comet to scour the Baths of Caracalla and inhaled so much ammonia we were lighter than air.

The hardest part of the whole routine, for me, was facing the icy dawn.

It was fortunate for everyone that Ken's faulty metabolism led him to leap from our bed at the first streak of daylight, as cheerful as if he'd slept until noon. Dawn, to Ken, is the time the world is reborn.

Dawn to me is the time when Indians creep up on wagon trains. When men face firing squads. Owls stalk rabbits. The moribund die. Mole-eyed milkmen make their rounds. Dawn is the time I want to burrow under the blankets and postpone reality for another year.

It was Ken who was sole producer of the titillating early-morning lodge smells of hot muffins, black walnut bread, pineapple streusel, and good hefty coffee. Daily I rolled over in our warm bed and thanked my stars I'd married an insomniac who could cook.

But only for an added forty minutes. The Gatling gun-fire of ski boots on slate floors heralded each new day—the result of an erroneous theory that to get properly encased in one's ski boot it was necessary to physically batter the boot into submission. This magpie racket transpired in the front corner of our upstairs lounge known as boot storage, an area equipped with wide shelves for overnight storage and drying of boots, and with long leather benches for the exchange of ski and after-ski footwear. The noise would have made a deaf-mute's hair bristle like Brillo. At the end of the first year I swore to replace that accursed flagstone flooring with solid foam rubber. But eventually, although not wholly inured, I grew hardened to the upstairs clatter; to the noise of six children being fueled, equipped, and dispatched to a throbbing, burping school bus; to jangling telephones; and to clangorously insouciant skiers. Sleeping in a ski lodge is like trying to snooze through a Concorde landing.

This morning pandemonium always rendered me partially stunned. I was never cranky, you understand, only comatose. Without Ken I never would have survived the start of each new day.

Ken, with the help of Ellie and Jake, got the wheels turning and ovens baking, while I slumped in a corner lugubriously swallowing coffee and my resentments. Just as I started to resemble one of the Hills Brothers, the coffee would finally grab hold and snap me to attention.

As the work force labored without me to mix juices, clear away the lounge debris from last night's drinkers, start roaring fires, bring in fresh wood, check the furnace, thaw out laundry room pipes, plow snow from the driveway, answer the telephones and start serving breakfast, I would write haphazard notes to teachers, learn with horror that I must make costumes for a school play opening the day after tomorrow, search frantically for milk money, talk two children out of leaving school forever and suffer terrible sinking spells.

After the Bernard Stapleton Memorial Bus Line had blessedly wafted away eight-tenths of our children, I would stagger up to the lounge to contribute my own distinctive note of false cheer. I supplied guests with trail and weather information as well as goggles, Band-Aids, boot laces, extra sweaters, and other equipment from our reserves, and helped chauffeur skiers to three different areas. (Despite all clarion-clear announcements, one person was invariably forgotten and the trip to be made all over again.) Eventually I was even able to join the headlong dashes between dishwasher, buffet sideboard, office, ski mountains, and back again.

With the relief of a man on parole, Ken bussed me on

the cheek and fled for the safe harbor of the Stein Eriksen Ski School. Then after every last man, woman, and child had clumped off and away, the Mr. Clean team started on the beds, baths, lounge, and kitchen with vacuum cleaners, mops, brooms, and sponges. I would pause to choke down a bite of lunch, prepare a tray for our sick or injured and play a few hands of gin with the patients. After that I made doctors' appointments and dinner reservations. Then I drove to town for the mail and guests' shopping needs which included: *Newsweek*, ski socks size twelve, safety pin packets, hair spray medium, airmail stamps, *The New York Times* three days late, emery boards, and needlepoint yarn. I bought the usual carload of groceries. Checked the Chamber. Came home. Drove back to Ajax to pick up a lodger who'd broken a ski. Home again. Then to Buttermilk for a child who'd lost a parent.

Back at the lodge I prepared après-ski appetizers, started the gluehwein, found wrappings to mail dozens of items left behind by departed skiers, flicked a dust kitty from under a table, misted the lemon tree, trimmed a week-old hangnail, began dinner preparations and looked up to see the first skiers lumbering down our driveway. Am I going too fast for you?

Despite these frenzied preliminaries, the period between four and six o'clock was my shining hour. The Heatherbed took on the character of a college rap session, and I had by now recovered my lark-like disposition.

I introduced newcomers, sympathized with skiers' block and clucked over the treacheries of the Elevator Shaft and Corkscrew. Our guests gathered together chattering, "Magnë finally straightened out my turn to the left." "Well, I flamed out on Bingo Slot again." "The patrol had two broken legs on Prospector in one hour." "If anyone ever points me down another trail like Exhibition I'm gonna take my marbles and go home." "Wow, I won my silver skis in the time trials."

By now Ken and some of his instructor cronies would

have joined the party, which he is always the life of. The skiing day fully rehashed, more drinks were downed, and plans for the evening finalized. "We're counting on everyone to join us for margaritas later." "Don't forget, Ken, you and Martie are our guests for dinner tonight at the Golden Horn."

Somehow we managed to chat with everyone, phone eighteen dinner reservations in to nine different restaurants, feed the children, call the hospital for a report on our spiral fracture, arrange dates for two darling Swarthmore students, have some of the men carry our pulled ligament into the lounge, note that our attractive divorcée had been invited to join a dinner group, dispense first aid, find last-minute space so those two nice people from Michigan wouldn't suffer exposure, ferry our guests out on the supper circuit, introduce the patrolmen and Vikings who'd stopped by for a drink, pose for Polaroid enthusiasts and love every minute of it.

Ken always said it was the Phyllis Diller taint coming out in me. He said I considered every night a first act curtain.

This was not, however, the grand finale.

Since many of our guests did not drive to Aspen, busing proved a bigger problem than the Supreme Court ever dreamed. Before we were finished, we had provided enough transportation to start a European invasion. Everyone over sixteen (and, in emergencies, certain underaged children) took turns driving guests in and around town; to and from ski shops, ski areas, and ski doctors; to night spots and eateries; to pick up friends in bars, luggage at the airport, and wives at the hairdresser's. The incessant jumping up and down and popping in and out gave our mornings and evenings the urgent air of a Navy flight deck preparing for attack.

The good Lord had blessedly arranged my union with Ken so that as he faded, I bloomed. Often he dozed off while we dined with guests or made up a table of bridge.

Just as he had taken over the dawn patrol, I was happy to fill in during his late-night lapses.

After hosting parties, showing ski movies, or escorting new arrivals around town (I always felt that, without our guidance, guests would wander the streets falling into tourist traps and missing the *real* Aspen), we infrequently crept into bed before midnight—usually to be aroused by someone needing a room, Bromo-Seltzer, painkillers, extra pillows, or an alto for harmonizing.

Teetering along this tightrope twenty-four hours a day had left us little time for leisure and me none at all for skiing. At the end of that first fallow period in January, I was as dazed as a playwright who's just survived fifteen rewrites, five out-of-town openings, and a Broadway first night.

CHAPTER 10

Show Time

I WAS diligently at work on some new package plan brochures, when Ken and the children began prodding me to go skiing while we had a lull. Doltishly I said, "Skiing?" as if it were something from the Sanskrit.

The children had not only been skiing over the holidays, weekends, and nights (down the driveway, jumping our steep embankments under the lodge lights), but also every Wednesday afternoon when masochistic housewives served as volunteer instructors. On Wednesday mornings the children gathered together ski poles, skis, mittens, liners, parkas, hats, boots, and socks amid the whimperings of a beleaguered mother and the bellowings of an outraged father.

"You kids swore to me you had everything all laid out and in order last night."

"We did, Dad, but that creep Gwendy copped my poles again."

"Those aren't yours, moron, they're mine. You left yours at ski team practice last weekend."

"One of the boys in school took my mitten. I told you that yesterday," Dede said tearfully through her hiccups.

"If you don't keep that lard-ass Daniel out of my things, Mom..."

"Please, Whit."

And so on and so on, amid cries of indignation and freshets of weeping from Deirdre of the Sorrows.

Bernard Stapleton, who drove our school bus with the equanimity of Saint John the Divine, had long since taken to parking the bus, grabbing a cup of coffee and pitching in to give the children a hand. It wasn't legal, and there was a slight stink from the PTA, the School Board, and one of the stuffier town fathers. But Bernard's service was the most personalized I expect to encounter this side of the River Styx, and we never could have made it through elementary school without him.

Eventually, under threat of bodily harm, the children became adroit at cornering and guarding every last piece of ski gear they owned—so adroit that I was reduced to creeping into their bedrooms in the dark of night to extract the filthy ski sweater a child had cached under his mattress so that I might wash and dry it before morning.

On weekends, the kids sped through their chores so they could meet friends on the mountain or report for ski team practice. Someone always volunteered to tote Danny over to the hill.

Then Robin, Mike, and Whit began skiing professionally at night.

Our friend Walt Smith owned the Hindquarter Restaurant at the Highlands. Above the restaurant was a lovely firelit after-supper club called the Freddie Fisher Room. There skiers were entertained by Walt's piano; by Freddie's ribald clarinet, alto sax, and repartee; and by King Fisher's trumpet. On the off chance that diners might become bored with Dixieland, prime beef, firelight, candlelight, and gemütlichkeit, the Hindquarter also featured torchlight, in a breathtaking after-dark descent of the mountain. This show, viewed through three levels of glass, was pretty spectacular. It was also a pain for the participants. It takes expertise to ski at night without poles while juggling two burning torches that not only cast deceptive shadows but also drip molten sparks on exposed wrists and perfectly good ski pants.

The backbone of this nocturnal ballet was the Highlands ski patrol, frequently accompanied by their girl friends. They were paid with free dinners and all they could drink, which made for a cheap as well as stimulating date. The trouble was that after a hard day hauling stretchers, the patrolmen were sick of those slopes and raring to tie one on. Not surprisingly, the torchlights grew increasingly sloppy.

One evening Walt called frantically to ask if any of our children could fill in—four of the patrol were too gassed to climb on the lift. My unequivocal answer was "No."

"It's only down Thunderbowl, Martie," he pleaded. "Listen, I've seen those kids ski. They're not only great, they're built too close to the ground to fall. Couldn't you send Jake along? We'll put them in the middle of the line. Everyone will go slow."

"No."

"It would be good for their balance," their father suggested unhelpfully.

"I'm desperate," wailed Walter. "The place is packed and people are clamoring for the torchlight."

"Weeeellll, just this one time," I relented grudgingly.

Jake went along as road manager and reported that the children skied without a slip, waving flares as jauntily as football pennants.

Thereafter the kids were in great demand. They dined early at home, stayed sober and left immediately following the seven o'clock performance to finish their homework. I never really approved. But every time Walt called in a choked-up voice, I surrendered once again and the children pulled old jeans over their ski pants for fire protection, bundled against the cold and trundled across the road to serve as a makeshift corps de ballet.

The children and their father had been coming home from the ski slopes bronzed and glowing for weeks. I looked like something recently pried from a clam shell, nacreously pale. Finally, Ken insisted it was my turn, that we were going to ski together while ski school was in limbo, and that he wouldn't take no for an answer. He adjusted the bindings on my new Kästles and oiled my dusty boots, and I climbed into my Christmas ski clothes, as ill at ease as though I were modeling for Givenchy.

The girls at the Highlands ticket office were glad to meet me at last, having no doubt decided that all those children had sprung full-blown from the pages of the J.C. Penney catalogue. I was issued my crisp new free ski pass, which I can tell you did a lot to remove the sting from that big, cancerous lodge mortgage, and Ken and I headed for the chairlift.

Any chairlift anywhere in the ski world is scenically eye-filling. But this lift had an extra added attraction. This scenery, this mountain, this lift were, in a sense, *ours.*

As we climbed past the lift towers clinging tenuously to the sides of the Stein Eriksen Run, we turned to watch the Heatherbed dwindling away to a Monopoly-sized hotel below. Smoke from our chimney fire drifted up like Indian talk. The lodge in its clearing was a picture of greeting-card tranquillity. Ken and I held hands, and I was as thrilled as if we'd struck oil and were gazing into our very own gusher.

Winter in Aspen does not mean the drab, gray cessation of life experienced in drearier climes. It means a sparkling rebirth amid new snow glitter and blazing sunshine, magnificent beyond telling. The snow transforms the mountains into gently carved rises, dips, hollows, and mounds—dollops of ice cream covering the harsh realities of bare earth. Here and there mine tailings drip like chocolate syrup down a white shirt front. There are few acute angles or brittle edges in snow country. Horizons are rounded, trees become soft sculpture. And everywhere, on a bright day, refracted light dances in a million prisms.

The sun is so blindingly near in high, thin air that it's *caveat emptor.* Without sunglasses, the skier's eyes can be damaged. Without skin protection, he can incur burns far more serious than those of the tropics. There is danger in the dazzle of Colorado country.

Just as lovely, in a very different way, are those days when a soft snow like the mists and whorls of London fog envelops the ski world. This is the time of so-called flat light, when there is no delineation between earth and sky and a skier becomes as weightless and disoriented as a man in space. With apocryphal guideposts and the hazes of the high Himalayas enveloping him, spiny urchins and the Lake Mead monster loom on his peripheral vision. All is eerily silent. He is as alone in the whiteout as Florence Chadwick in a channel fog.

Expert skiers love the challenge of flat light. They switch to instrument flying and, abetted by sure instincts and strong thighs, flex their knees to absorb the sudden shocks of unseen bumps, moving joyously, blindly down through the unknown. The novice feels a sudden queasiness, finds his knees bouncing up to smack his chin and is as dazed as a wanderer in a hall of mirrors.

On flat light days, we who are not experts take to the cross-country trails, where the undulating world is a billowing comforter, broad perspective unimportant, the enormous silence a silken luxury.

Ken pointed out the tracks of snowshoe rabbits, ermine, porcupines, of birds, coyote, elk, and deer—their crisscrossing of new snow as symmetrical as feather stitching on a colonial quilt. Many of the trees were stripped of bark by porkies, and a "bear tree" marked the spot where a local family of black bears regularly sharpened their claws to signal territorial claims. Beneath us, surrounding the triple A-frames of the Highlands base house, trout ponds gleamed in the morning sunlight. From this height we could pick out the abrupt cutoffs where glacial moraine had ceased its carving of our deep, cliff-girt valley.

"Oh, darling," I breathed in a voice out of a Gothic

novel, "I'd forgotten how beautiful it is. Everything simply radiates purity."

"Not me. I'm hot for your skinny body," said my husband, giving me a cold, tingly kiss. I was so pleased I nearly choked up.

On my first day as a skiing native, it was intoxicating just knowing there would be weeks, months, and years to absorb any sensation I missed that day or the next. I knew how Zebulon Pike, Tenzing Norkay, and Sir Edmund Hillary must have felt—only *I* could return to my mountain top again and again.

We skied high up and far around, ending above the Thunderbowl, where the U.S. Olympic girls were practicing slalom runs. From our vantage point they looked like miniature gladiators feinting and sparring and darting among brightly flagged poles.

Beyond them the Roaring Fork Valley spread to the northwest. On our right balanced the Sundeck, a glistening epaulet on the shoulder of Ajax. To the left, Buttermilk's bowls shimmered like gargantuan vats of junket. Around us rose Aspen's mountains, each with its own singularity, its own weather.

I followed Ken until my face stretched taut with sun- and windburn, and my legs quaked with fatigue. Finally we fell into the bierstube, where I downed two ambrosial ales but was too exhausted to eat. Then Ken supported my tottering frame across the road.

I count it as one of the red-letter days of my life.

The demolished mother of the corps de ballet had not, at this point, seen one of her children ski. Oh, I saw them dressing, undressing, coming, going and jumping the driveway. But I had never yet seen them descend a bona fide ski slope.

The Highlands was designed as a family area, with a central base house where clans gathered, and children swarmed like litters of wriggling puppies. I had content-edly visualized our baby ballerinas attending classes (ad-mittance free for instructors' children); learning to stand on skis, walk on skis, snowplow on skis; and cavorting and frolicking about the beginner slopes. When Uncle Whit kissed us good-bye the Friday following New Year's Eve, he said, "You'd better ski with those children, Martie. They're going to pass you like runaway locomotives. You'll never see their smoke again."

Later I stared moodily at our spawn and their para-phernalia scattered the length and breadth of the apart-ment. I wondered wistfully what life in a beach resort would have been, with each child requiring exactly two skimpy bathing suits and possibly three or four baths *per year*. It's tough to take pride in your progeny when you face the equivalent of a 5.4 earthquake on the Richter scale every time they suit up for action.

"I'm tickled to hear our little darlings are faster than firehorses," I said to the room at large. "But do you sup-pose there's enough strength in those rapid-fire bodies to clear a path for foot traffic and the table for dinner? Or am I expected to assist our future champions to their places and administer a massage with the first course?" (This was the way Wednesdays, Saturdays, and Sundays went that first year.)

DearGwen said eagerly, "We'll pick up the mess, Mother."

Mike volunteered, "I'll make salad for dinner."

"Dibs on setting the table," Dede called.

"Oh for cripe's sake, I'll take the dishes," Whit ac-quiesced good-naturedly.

I looked at them as though they'd just told me the ski team was a front for the Cosa Nostra. "Hey, what is this, guys? Am I being blackmailed?"

"You bet your sweet patootie," grinned Whit.

"Oh, we want you to go skiing, mother," Robin pleaded.

"You've been promising and promising," they all cho-rused.

"Me too," Danny piped up from under a pile of parkas, where he was curled with three dogs and a cat. "Me too" seemed to cover Dan's needs from toilet to table. I worried that his vocabulary might be stunted.

The next morning I bumbled out of bed, put a venison roast on to a simmer, struggled into uniform, picked up the baby blue Kästles, assembled the children in squad formation, and off we marched like a military Mother Goose and six noncommissioned goslings.

This first expedition *en famille* was, I'll admit it, a thrill. A mackerel sky was shimmering, the sun again caressing, the day heaven-sent. Overflowing with mother's warmth, I inwardly rehearsed those pointers I felt would be helpful to the children.

We clumped up the wooden stairs beside the ski shop.

"Hi, Stein," called Whit.

"Allo, Whit. You giffing a lesson tewday, eh? And big Dan too. We take a run later, yah?"

"I can do that kick turn like you showed us," Mike called back as we tromped onward.

"What on earth is a kick turn?" I asked absentmindedly. "And who was that?"

"We'll show you the turn, it's keen. That was Stein," said Gwendy.

"Stein who?"

"You know, *our* Stein."

"Good grief, Stein Eriksen?" I hadn't yet met the man, but heaven knew I'd heard plenty of advance publicity.

"Don't lose your cool, Mother. You're puffing like a steam engine," Robin said solicitously. As an afterthought she added, "That man sure has improved our skiing. Maybe he'll give you some pointers too."

I couldn't have been more taken aback if the children had informed me that nice Mr. Einstein down the street was helping them with New Math.

Suddenly I stopped in midstride toward the general area of the T-bar. Cautiously I inquired, "Exactly where have you been receiving all this classic instruction, my dears?"

"Oh, the older kids ski Exhibition, . . ." said Gwen.

". . . but Gwendy and Dan and I go to the top in the chair and run Ego Alley, till we get more parallel," finished Dee.

"Mother of God," I whispered. "But children, those are *expert* trails."

They looked at me kindly.

"You *are* sorta out of shape, Mother. Maybe we could all mess around the T-bar while you warm up," Whit offered generously.

"Well, er . . ."

"Holy cow, we don't really expect you to keep up, you being rusty and older and all," Mike said.

I had the abrupt sensation that, less than one-third of the way through our first ski season, I had been eclipsed by a bunch of wet-nosed kids. I would have been happier having it happen in slow, temporal stages. But then who was I to stay the stampede of progress?

"I'm right behind you, gang," I assured them with false heartiness as we picked up our passes, strapped on our skis, tacked to the right and headed for the world's longest double chairlift.

"Let's take turns riding with Mom, me first," called Whit.

"Who gets Danny this trip?" someone asked.

"What do you mean, who gets him?" spake the unnerved parent.

Robin explained, "We take turns riding with him. He's not reliable."

Since Danny's fourth birthday was not until April, I couldn't have agreed more. Reliability was only one of the sterling qualities he had not developed, along with sense, balance, and judgment. However, looking into the trusting faces of his siblings, I could see the other children believed in him, and that was a plus.

"I'll take Dan with me," I volunteered. "Whit dear, the next ride is yours."

I was relieved when the lift operators greeted the children with that familiarity reserved for immediate members of the family. And when they slowed the lift to a halt and assisted Daniel up into the chair. (His legs were too short to bridge the gap.) But I had not previously noted that this lift had no guardrail. And that it jiggled alarmingly across a number of fifty-foot drops. While a squirming, impatient male child threatened every minute to drop mittens, poles, or scarf and forgetfully dive out after them, I suffered the worst case of paresis I'd had since Independence Pass.

Wriggling in my iron-glove grip, Danny informed me, "Mom, I hafta go to the baffroom."

"Sssssh. Don't talk now, baby. And hold on very tight until we get across this great big ditch."

"I know howta hang on, mom, but I hafta whizz."

"Well, what do you usually do when you must go to the bathroom up here?"

"First the guys get mad. Then they put me behind a tree."

"I can scarcely put you behind a tree in midair, buddy, now can I?" I half expected to hear that his resourceful brethren adjusted his pants and tilted him toward a passing lift tower in this predicament.

"No, but you can tell me a funny stowy and take my mind offa it."

Over the remainder of the winter I was to have a lion's share of telling Dan stories, putting him behind trees and barring the front of the chair as casually as possible with a ski pole. (After the day of the Great Exposé, I watched over that three-year-old like a mother hawk. It didn't do much for my skiing, but it was a great help to my peace of mind.)

My feeling that children at that tender age are too young to ski remains unchanged. The youngest of six is apt to have other ideas. Dan had refused from the crib to be left behind, and the older children, although sometimes impatient, were surprisingly sympathetic. I could never understand why. A three-year-old on a ski mountain is without fear or sense, has chronically weak kidneys, and is a big fat millstone around everyone's neck.

As I sang "Hut sut ralston on the rillera" for the wriggling babe, our children's voices rang out from the chairs. "Hi, Arnë," "Yo, Magnë," "Coolsville, Steinthør."

Beneath us Arnë, Magnë, Steinthør, et al, raised heads from ski classes, waved poles, called out greetings.

"Well. You certainly do know everyone on the mountain," I said to the children when, another kindly operator having stopped the lift to set Danny down, we all dismounted and assembled at the top.

"We spend half our lives here, Mother, we ought to. Don't worry. We'll introduce you to everybody."

"Weady?" called Dan from the lip of the slight headwall where he was coiled over his skis, poles dug in, ready for shove-off—a small, fat quilted bird of prey.

"We always let him lead off, it makes him feel like Steve Reeves," Robin whispered out of the corner of her mouth.

"Weady, mom?" repeated Steve Reeves.

"Lead off, I'll follow," I called. I have been following, from a greater and greater distance, ever since.

By the end of our first season Mike and Whit were traveling to five states for four-way meets, winning junior slaloms, leaping off sixty-meter jumps (an event I watched once and thereafter arranged to be excused from), proudly accepting their first trophies and hobnobbing with the likes of TV's Matt Dillon.

Soon I would learn that ski car pools in the West meant driving to Idaho in the morning and to New Mexico next weekend. Skiing mothers are far less flinty than skating mothers. It's because they're tired all the time.

The children have remained gracious about inviting their aged mother to ski. However, I realize the sacrifice this has entailed. For years I have compromised by skiing with another crone or two and then meeting the kids for lunch. This way we are all on an equal footing, hungry, and I get to pay the bill.

That first revelatory Saturday, Danny went into a snowplow so "spraddled" that his bottom scraped the snow. Since he had not yet learned the art of turning, he simply headed straight down the mountain. Two- and three-year-olds are one-half library paste and one-half India rubber, so he was never even bruised. At ten he was addressed by coach Teddy Armstrong as "Downhill Dan, first in our hearts, last in the seed." At twenty he had grown past six feet, was taking seventy-foot headers as a downhill racer and was the only one of the children never to have broken a leg. Maybe there's something to be said for starting from the ground up after all.

Over lunch I discovered that the children were not only on intimate terms with the lift operators, the ski patrolmen, Stein, and all of his instructors, but also with a number of attractive Sun Belters who owned vacation homes in Aspen and cattle empires down home. Also with several bored widow ladies who did not ski, but spent their afternoons on the Highlands sundecks getting a tan, clipping coupons and lying in wait for young children to spoil. Spoiling young children consisted of stuffing them with hot chocolate, cheeseburgers, and indigestible pastries.

"Listen, you guys," I hissed. "I want you to stop cadging food and drinks."

"It's mostly the boys who do it," Robin declared indignantly.

"Okay, men, after skiing we're going to have a nice long heart-to-heart."

The boys groaned. Heart-to-hearts meant I did the talking and they experienced disciplinary action.

Just then Stein came to our table, introduced himself, bought me a drink, commented graciously, and at length, on the manners and charm of all the children and took the wind right out of my sails.

I answered weakly, "Well, resort life is a change, but they certainly seem to have adjusted."

"Boy, have they adjusted," I snapped later at Ken and Jake. "And with the full connivance of you two snakes in the snow. You've known all along that they've been living off the fat of tourists, bombing that mountain from the top and taking Danny on that horrible lift."

"Well, yes, honey, but . . ."

"Ever since Thanksgiving I've thought they were 'futzing around' on Thunderbowl and those nice, gentle beginners' slopes. If I'd known the truth, I wouldn't have permitted any of this for a minute." (I was beginning to sound like Angelo Dundee in the ring.)

"Exactly, dear. And that's why we . . ."

"Kenneth Robinson Sterling, you and your first sergeant have deliberately deceived the overwrought mother of a large family," I sputtered.

Ken grinned complacently and said, "Try to collect yourself, Martie. By the time those children are racing Downhill on the F.I.S., no one will remember that it wasn't you who gave them their start."

CHAPTER 11

Culture Shock

JANUARY ON the ski front may have been as dead as the surfboard franchise in Fairbanks, but I wouldn't say it was dull.

When Scott and Elaine Linge arrived from Fayette, Iowa, they were our only guests. "Then why is it," Scott asked dazedly, "that this place is buzzing like a political convention?" I couldn't explain it myself. Maybe it was all the kids and dogs. Or Claytie's armies of whacko friends. Or because all of Aspen was frenetically preparing for our annual celebration of the snow, Winterskol.

We liked the Linges and they liked us, and it was a good thing because we were soon together every waking moment they weren't skiing. We dragged them to parties and Winterskol meetings, and even introduced them to the horse business.

Although it was Ken who'd made our long-range plans for summer pack trips, breakfast rides, and other horsey attractions, the opening round was unexpectedly mine.

I'd been seated next to Storrs Bishop at a Chamber of Commerce meeting discussing the January doldrums and, as I confessed to Ken, "He has this pair of harness horses just standing around the barn doing nothing all winter, and one thing led to another and . . . "

"Listen, Martie, just because I worked on the Pennsylvania National Horse Show for ten years doesn't mean I know a hoof from a hock!" Ken roared after Storrs called to say he'd be out the next day with Mollie Gibson and Annie Malone. (Two rather tacky old mares named for burned-out mine claims, which should have told me something.)

"But Storrs knows everything about horses, he'll teach you and Jake all about harness and tack, and we do have that great big corral all fenced for McDuff that he's rattling around in like a lone marble, and I thought if we had some nice jangling sleigh bells and painted a lacy sign with the lodge name on it and trotted around town giving people free rides it would sort of remind them of St. Moritz and be wonderful advertising, and we could drive our guests to town and . . ." Ken's face was as thunderous as a bank of cumulus mammatus, and I had run out of breath and excuses.

"What a royal bunch of crap. We'll have the horses in the ditch, the sleigh upside down, and ourselves in front of county court."

"But sweetheart, you *did* plan on horses this spring, and Storrs says it's a cinch to learn about harnessing, it only takes a lit-tle work."

"Dammit, I wish you'd discuss decisions involving *my* work and *my* neck and *Jake's* back and *his* work with Jake and me instead of Storrs. You can call him right back and tell him to take his Mollie and his Annie and his cockleshells and jingle bells and stuff them into the nearest stable until summer."

"I can't."

"What's more, I—what the hell do you mean you can't?"

The children were wide-eyed. They had seldom seen their convivial father so deranged.

"Boy, he's mad enough to chew nails," Whit whispered.

"He's already taken a good chunk out of Mom," Robin quaked.

"Wanna hear a neat riddle?" asked DearGwen hopefully.

"You'd better cool it, he's sore as a crab," Dee said in an awed tone.

I drew a deep breath. "Ken, I gave Storrs half of our grocery money for a month's lease on those horses."

"Oh, my Lord in heaven, I am going to run away and join the Mafia."

The next afternoon Ken, coached dolorously by Scott Linge, nailed up extra corral railings. His burping, always his private stress indicator, had reached the proportions of Hell's Angels backfire. Storrs meanwhile was explaining the mysteries of hames, bits, buckles, and harness to Jake, who was secretly elated at his new role as stage driver/mule skinner. He had adopted a battered cowboy hat left behind by Ed Cain, picked up some ancient canvas chaps at the thrift shop, and was soon "gee-hawing" and "whoaing" the great, shaggy, winter-coated mares as if he'd been born to the wagon seat.

I felt more than a little subdued before all that bristling, prancing, jangling tonnage that threatened momentarily to break out of Jake's muscular grasp and trample us underfoot. As for McDuff, he'd retreated to a rear corner of the corral, where he glared in outrage at the invasion of his territory.

"They're lazy right now," Storrs shouted over the snorting and pawing. "They've been soaking up Omaline and corn in the barn, and they need to take some weight off. But they'll frisk up plenty after Jake puts them through their paces."

"Oh, but they're just dandy the way they are," I assured him hastily. "Er, aren't they sort of *large*?"

"Part Belgian," Storrs stated proudly. "You need a big hefty pair when you're hauling a sleigh and payload."

"Bet they eat a lot," Ken called from the fence, where

he was cursing another hammered finger and his *persona non grata* wife.

"I've brought you fourteen bales for starters. They'll last you maybe a week. Just be sure to grain 'em plenty and put molasses in their feed. When they're working, they need a lot of fuel."

"How much is hay going for a ton?" Ken inquired, glowering balefully at me.

"Paid fifty dollars last month. A little dear this winter, what with the dry summer."

At dinner that night Ken nattered endlessly about the price of hay and Omaline and corn. "When we've paid the bills for the horse feed," he said chattily to the children, "we can farm you kids out as apprentices. Get someone else to feed and clothe you through the winter while you learn a trade."

"Ken!"

"Your ding-a-ling mother has taken the food out of your mouths and put it into those two wild-eyed monsters. And they aren't even members of this family."

The children were blithely unconcerned about their next meal and deliriously happy at adding such enormous pets to their menagerie. It was evident they already considered their hamsters tedious.

"They can have my dinner," Dan announced, eagerly pushing aside his green beans.

"Ours too," echoed Dee and Gwendy. "We won't eat much."

"Oh, for heaven's sake," sighed Ken. "Let's not have an outbreak of malnutrition on account of a couple of old bay mares . . . Outflanked again," he added to me and managed a small, feeble grin.

As pre-Winterskol flew by, Ellie, the children, and I spent long hours transforming Jens Christiansen's flatbed wagon into what we hoped would be a winning float. We were entering as "The Threadbare Lodge—No Service Too Skimpy."

We erected a big old brass bed billowing with comforters on the wagon, and Ken sweet-talked Fred Fisher out of a prized secondhand toilet and bathtub plus an antique wood-burning stove, all modishly arranged as complete hotel facilities afloat. Ken, nattily attired in long red underwear, was to be enthroned with a copy of the Sears, Roebuck catalogue and a large supply of corncobs. I'd made Victorian chambermaid dresses and aprons and floppy mobcaps for the girls, who would carry feather dusters and signs saying "Up to the minute room service"; Dan would be attired in a tucked-up instructor's uniform, his sign, "Private Ski Instruction"; Whit and Mike were to be top-hatted chimney sweeps. And we prayed fervently for some raffish guests to join the Linges in the bathtub and bed with all the dogs, who would wear sequined ski goggles (they already had the furs) as chichi ski jetters.

Freddie said, "You can borrow the tub and toilet, but I don't approve of it. Those are some of my best pieces, and I don't want you cracking 'em."

Actually Freddie had a very commodious barn and backyard overflowing not only with bathroom fixtures but also with stoves, car parts, cars, bicycles, antiques, tools, billboards, horse troughs, donkey engines, old tires, birdbaths, statuary, moving parts, and general junk. So much of it that I couldn't conceive how he'd ever miss two or three paltry pieces of plumbing. Freddie's business was barter.

Freddie "Schnickelfritz" Fisher had preceded Spike Jones as the musical lunatic of the Thirties, had appeared in many movies with Rudy Vallee and had traveled the world as a top entertainer. Touring cross-country, he'd come down with flat tires in Glenwood Springs and wandered over to Aspen for a look while they were repaired. He never left.

Freddie's accountant of many years had only recently left him holding the bag and a subpoena from the IRS.

Since Freddie was a free spirit uninterested in a life spent in federal courts or correctional institutions, he had been claiming, rightfully, to be flat broke ever since. He now survived in conjugal comfort without ever fingering a piece of hard cash. He played every woodwind and brass instrument known to the orchestra; electroplated aspen leaves with a secret formula devised "by Freddie Fisher and God"; and strolled around town like a Bowery derelict scrounging, swapping and trading.

Marge Fisher smiled fondly at Fred, at his Durante nose and home-designed false teeth, and said, "He gave me enough mink stoles and fancy hotel suites for a lifetime when I was young. You don't need those things when you're older."

"Trade you for one of those sheepskin coats," Fred would growl around a toothpick to a local merchant. Or, "Tell you what, Ken. I'll fix your lock and you can just swap me some of that extra venison in your freezer."

Freddie was an Original: jazz musician *extraordinaire*, amateur physician, artist, inventor, Mr. Fix-it, Moslem rug merchant—all rolled into one eccentric package.

As Winterskol neared, Freddie kept popping by to make certain his plumbing was covered against the night air and to commiserate with Ken as Mollie and Annie chomped hay nonstop. The two men could be seen leaning on the corral fence chatting in low, mournful tones.

"Damn women'll do it to you every time."

"At these prices we should be eating hay," Ken groaned.

"Just wait'll one of 'em comes down with encephalitis."

Ken blanched. "They wouldn't dare."

"They look kinda scraggly to me. Say, son, did I ever tell you about the time I peed on a skunk?"

"No!"

"He hightailed it clean out of the yard. Mebbe you and I should try pissin' on those horses."

*   *   *

Well, our bank balance may have been lower than a snake's belly, but as the Linges said, we *looked* busy. Jake became more venturesome with the sleigh by the hour. Claytie, who was decorations chairman for the Winterskol Ball, ran around with her hair pinned up, clipboards in both hands, absentmindedly bumping into furniture and Mrs. Packard. Lapis cigarette holder dangling from her mouth, she squinted through clouds of smoke that would have gagged Paul Henreid and Bette Davis. Uncle Whit arrived for weekends with Denver skiing buddies. Jake brought processions of good-looking girls home for dinner. Ellie turned up every Bostonian for miles. The Vikings and their friends were in and out. The Linges joined the family for good. The children's friends milled about. The dogs wrestled joyously in the snow. And the Belgians and McDuff munched pastorally on the last of our Christmas profits.

Looking at all those burstingly healthy bodies was enough to revive my Depression nightmares of the poorhouse.

Listen, I sympathize with today's young workers who must hold two jobs to survive in the high-rent district Aspen's become. But twenty-five years ago there *weren't* two jobs, and things were a lot more critical. To make the grade everyone watered the soup, ate elk they'd shot, trout they'd hooked, garden stuff they'd grown. We also lived on credit extended by Tom's Market and Beck & Bishop through the interminable off-seasons. By the time Christmas came around, I was sure we'd be jailed for spending all the advance guest deposits.

We were so desperate that, when our guests sent us large, festive looking packages, we'd frenziedly tear them apart, praying for a smoked turkey, a fruitcake, an assortment of cheeses, or a sack of pecans. I don't know about other lodge owners, but our surprise packages usually contained ten gallons of Prestone (from a morose garageman), cartons of coat hangers (a concerned dry cleaning manager), wholesale lots of cosmetics (Jesse Bell, Bonnie Bell cosmetics), cases of tiki torches (Tiki John Freiburg), cartons of remaindered books (a minor Philadelphia publisher), and wildly improbable gifts from lame-brains like Mrs. Packard. She sent us, as a Christmas thank you, a fifteen-foot pink balloon of satin and isinglass, bedizened with velvet streamers and many fake jewels. That little Neiman-Marcus bibelot must have cost a cool three hundred dollars. And we never did figure out where, or why, to float the idiot thing.

What I found most discouraging were the many sheaves of long-stemmed roses sent to us by grateful guests. They smelled of Persian gardens, were exquisite to look at, but we couldn't eat them. Despondently I looked into friary cookbooks and researched books on herbs for rose hip nostrums and rose petal poultices. I even tried them in soup. Years later, I still view roses the way mourners do funeral set pieces—with a concave feeling in the pit of my stomach.

What with one thing and another, the three kinds of pie I had served Ken in our youth were becoming a crepuscular thing of the past. Robin struggled manfully to close the gap. But the chronic shortage of money and time, plus sheer numbers, precluded a lot of baking binges. It would have required the output of a Twinkies factory simply to keep pace with the demand.

It was during this period that I began to feel that people, like animals, should be fed only once a day. As a result my meals were often served up without all of the finishing touches.

Given this state of very marginal survival, taking in a visiting ski team could be a real hardship. Just the same, we all did it. When the dinner roster expanded from ten to twenty-five, I simply added leaves to our large oak table, watered the spaghetti sauce and threw more beans in the chili.

I learned to make chili right and make it hot when the Chilean Olympic ski team, six strong and voracious as werewolves, moved in with us in mid-January.

The 1960 Winter Olympics, the first to be held in the United States since 1932, were coming to the new resort of Squaw Valley, California. Squaw's facilities and ski mountain would not be ready until the eve of opening ceremonies. Until then we, along with many Aspenites, welcomed any Olympians who wanted to use our snow. Ria had been boarding U.S. racers Penny Pitou and Betsy and Sunny Snite over at the Vagabond since November— at no charge of course. Families opened larders and guest rooms to skiers from Austria to Australia—at no charge of course. And at no charge the Heatherbed gathered to its straining bosom Jaime Hernandez, Rudolpho Esteban, Phillipe Sanchez, Perro Rodriguez, Lobo Concha, and Indio Pedregal.

My thoughts, if indeed I'd had any as I abstractedly said, "We'll be happy to help," were of doing our civic duty and possibly having someone for the children to practice their Spanish on. None of us had heard of culture shock. We would not have believed it if we had.

We felt its first tremor when the Chileans careened down our driveway crucifying a borrowed Jeep at sixty m.p.h. in low gear. As it belched, moaned, and finally clattered to a stop, an Olympic committeeman crept shakily from the back, introduced his charges and staggered straight to the office to call a cab. Meanwhile, Ken was the mortified recipient of many passionate *abrazos* and the backs of my hands were smothered in very moist kisses.

"Aqui iss uno beyootiful 'otel." "Señor, señora, our countree she say 'Gracias.'" "Our Madre de Dio, She say 'Gracias.'" "Si, si, muchas gracias." More hand-kissing. More *abrazos*.

The Chileans installed a makeshift flagpole and hoisted

their red, white, and green national colors above our entrance. Syrupy black eyes gazing deeply into mine, they borrowed my G.E. steam iron which they used to iron hot wax on their Pe-tex bottoms and returned with many ardent "tonk you's," more devouring gazes, and a thick residue of black scorch. They requested extra bed sheets, which they used to wrap their skis against sudden harmful temperature changes. They preempted dozens of perfectly good towels to apply polish, sealer, and beeswax to their precious ski boots. The only thing they emphatically did not borrow were our vehicles, which Ken stood ready to defend with his Allen wrench and dying breath.

The Chileans were Latin to their ski tips, down to and including the traditional Spanish death wish. They drove with hair-raising abandon and total disregard for vehicular law; skied with an unconstraint that sent hackers flailing for the trees; kissed any woman in sight even if she was pushing seventy and looked like a gerbil; and awakened everyone for miles singing tormentedly of heartbreak nights and joy-filled days.

The Chileans had a team battle cry which was later banned from the Olympic site—a chanted howl composed of equal parts Yma Sumac, Comanche war whoop, and the screech of tearing metal. Spurred on by our enthralled children, one of them would take up the opening beat: "Rrrrrrrrrum-bah, RRRRRRUUUUUUMMMM-MM-Bah, RRRRRRRUUUUUUUUUUM-Bah, Rrrrrru, rum, rum." This sound then broadened into a spine-chilling cry with overtones of Pict and Visigoth. They were joined on the choruses by all of our dogs, in whom The Cry aroused every ancestral strain of wolf.

Mrs. Packard's hum grew more full-bodied by the day. And of course Claytie was beside herself, chirping kitchen Spanish in imperfect syntax and piling the boys in and around her Mercedes to sweep off nightly and do the town. The Chileans called Claytie "Chichotas," and she called them "you dear baby savages," and every morning they came home howling, chanting and singing between three and five A.M.

"Claytie, those infants are supposed to be in training," I said indignantly.

"Oh, pooh. They're as strong as young bulls and they may never get back this way. It is my bounden duty to show them America from the inside out."

"I'll just bet it is. Inside your cozy bed and outside all the rules."

She had the grace to blush. "Martha Jane, you are such an old stick."

"And you, my friend, are old enough to be their mother."

"Not unless I was one of those eleven-year-old Peruvian child brides, you stinker!"

The Cry had originated with the boy Indio, who was not your routine Portillo or Santiago Chilean. He sprang from somewhere high in the Andes, was unadulterated Incan and didn't even speak Spanish.

Actually Indio never spoke at all. He simply looked alert, his button-black eyes moving from face to face and marking every exit in a room. When Indio had needs the other boys divined them. If he wished to vent his feelings, he broke into the Battle Cry. Indio at top speed was the fastest skier on the team, and Indio in full voice could single-throatedly set off an avalanche.

The Chileans plummeted up and down our drive and the ski runs like Mario Andretti gone daft, leered shamelessly at our Campfire Girl daughters, and triumphantly presented me with a housegift bouquet of live, unplucked chickens they'd wheedled out of a local rancher.

"Well, it *is* something to eat," I said a little woefully as Ken dunked naked poultry into boiling water, fur flew, and we painstakingly plucked out hundreds of pin feathers. "I'm so hungry for white meat, I thought of wringing their necks and devouring them raw," he sneezed.

Meanwhile, the children picked up quite a bit of Spanish, most of it unacceptable in polite homes. On weekends they followed the Chileans like peons trailing an Andalusian *hidalgo*. (It was influences of exactly this sort that led to Danny, only recently out of training pants, traveling to eleven thousand feet while I rested secure in the belief he was enrolled in kiddies' ski school far below.)

However, I had more immediate concerns.

Mother was headed for the mountains.

CHAPTER 12

Mother Comes to the Mountain

THE CABLE read: "Docking San Francisco from Hong Kong Friday. Meet Continental Flight #298 Denver, Saturday January 21, 3:00 P.M. Eager to see all. Love Mother."

I was the color of spackling compound as I hung up the phone. "Lord help us," I whispered. "She'll be here in less than two weeks. We've got exactly one room booked, and you know Mother, she can smell a deficit at fifty yards." I felt the complete despair of a family burned out of its home.

"I thought she hated cold weather and was waiting for the summer music festival," Ken said indignantly.

"Oh boy, Franny's coming," shouted the children. Mother is one of the world's great grandmothers. She makes me wish I'd started at the top, simply skipping all those burdensome gestation periods and diaper changes.

Mother had adapted to widowhood with her customary spunk. She took in the opera in New York, the sun in Florida, and a good bridge game anywhere in the world. This latest trip was a Charles Goren bridge cruise the length and breadth of Asia.

"Oh, Lord, we're not ready," I said, frenziedly eyeing the children, Ken, Claytie, our apartment, and the empty reservation charts.

Ken was his usual tower of strength. "What do you mean, ready? The lodge is up, the roof's on, we're warm."

"Ken, you'll just never understand these things. If I'd known Mother was coming I'd have cleaned the furnace . . . trimmed all the trees . . . mended the towels . . . bribed the weatherman and called out the Mounties." I was panting like a hunted animal.

Ken assumed his Lone Prairie expression and mused, "Why is it that when we hear from your mother it's like the howl of encircling wolves, I wonder?"

"Oh, stop it, Daddy, you aren't funny," Robin scolded.

"Boy, I can hardly wait," said Gwendy.

"We'll teach her to ski," Whit added.

"That's a hot one," snorted Ken.

"Well, but of course I'll entertain her, darlings," Claytie said, pursing her lips around a Fatima and shaking up another martini. "But it will be awkward. I'm up to my ovaries in this ball affair and . . . I know, I'll throw a nice rowdy milk punch party on Sunday morning, and everyone can bring his Winterskol hangover and sober up. Sliding Rock and his Slippery Rockers will be happy to play. Red can bring his boom bass, and . . ."

John "Sliding Rock" Locke, like Buffalo Bill, had hair over his scapulae and fringes to his knees. He and his Slippery Rockers were only slightly less rough-and-tumble than Elvis and his Hound Dawgs and not what you'd call Mother's cup of tea. I said agitatedly, "It's sweet of you to offer, Claytie dear, but Mother's been at sea for seven weeks and—"

"More like seventy years," muttered Ken.

"—and I think she'd appreciate just seeing the children and doing quieter things," I finished lamely.

"Now, Martha Jane, I do think you should reconsider. We'll be right on the Aquarian cusp, and Mrs. Packard just might get her act together and raise somebody to the roof for us." (Claytie had become more than mildly irritated with Mrs. Packard, who hadn't raised a thing but her eyebrows since the day they'd met.) Her eyes shone anticipatorily. "It would be the *succès fou* of the season."

Ken choked on a handful of peanuts and had to be pounded heartily on the back before he could regain speech. "If you knew Frances like I know Frances," he moaned deliriously. "She thinks any party without a receiving line and a string quartet is trashy."

"You keep out of this," I hissed. "Claytie dear, Mother is simply not the levitational type."

"Oh, very well, Martha Jane. You needn't spell it out. Your mother is a part-time Benedictine abbess, and you want me to be on my very best dancing school behavior."

"Oh, Claytie," I breathed. "If you could just promise no funny guests or monkeyshines. It really would make things so much easier." Up to this point Claytie had run afoul of and brought home: an oil portraitist who was "terribly talented but I can't get the stubborn baby to take a bath in anything except linseed oil"; Billie Brondizi, an international flake who was a paid companion to the poetess Mina Loy; Waldo Douglas Croydon, still homesteading a mine claim his grandfather had staked in 1887; a very funny, very ribald English comedian named Jonathon Moore; strays too drunk to find their cars or front doors; and a collection of Eastern religious fanatics, ne'er-do-wells, minor royalty, and nuts that would have stocked every sanatorium in the state.

"I will be the soul of tact, discretion, lavender, and old lace," Claytie promised.

I doubted it. There was a speculative gleam in those pale green eyes.

Winterskol festivities finally opened on a Thursday morning with the lodge ski race. By ten o'clock the snow that had fallen on Squaw Valley the night before had swept our way. I'd elected to gate-keep in one of the family raccoon coats that smelled of daguerreotypes and mothballs and the snow was falling so hard that I soon resembled a large, cumbersome polar bear.

Our lodge team was packed with family ringers: Half-Whit, Mike, Jake, and Ken. By the time everyone had gone back up Little Nell for the second run, the Heatherbed was leading by a good margin, and the snow was so driving we felt as if we were caught in a mechanized car wash. Our team needed only complete the course without falling. We almost didn't make it.

Whit was the last one to run, and if I hadn't heard his name over the loudspeaker, I never would have recognized the small snowball streaking my way. Damë had no such identity problems. As Whit neared the finish line, Dick Parker excitedly held up his stop watch and shouted, "He's going to make it, young Whit Sterling is going to bring the Heatherbed in at a healthy five seconds under the nearest time." Then I saw *two* flying balls of snow. With that special instinct of all beloved family pets, Damë had smelled her buddy and dashed onto the course to welcome him to the bottom. They collided, Whit crossed the finish line in midair, and we won the gold cup.

"It isn't a bad break," said Bob Oden, M.D. "Just a hairline fracture. I've casted him so he'll have full use of those fingers in school."

"Dullsville," murmured Whit sleepily.

"You can take him home. Just keep him quiet tonight. And you might consider shooting the dog," Bob said.

Whit's cast was soon covered with Messages from Garcia, and he was resting comfortably. Heaven knew the lodge was at the ready. In preparation for Mother I had scrubbed the carpeting with a toothbrush; fumigated our quarters with gallons of Lysol; cleaned the lint traps; washed every window until it blinded the naked eye; and mated all of the children's socks for the first time in a year.

There's something about a heavy snowfall that brings skiers streaming faster than lemmings to the sea. Ross and Nancy Grimes were to arrive the next morning for a long weekend. So would Gloria and John Rice from Colorado Springs. Harold and Gerry Carr had been staying in town, but after a preview peak at our parade float, they packed up their gear, moved out with us and insisted they get into the act. (Harold was a middle-aged pixie who'd succeeded in the tool and die business and on every yearly trip produced one silver dollar out of his ear for each delighted child.) Then Lee Uris and Tiki John Freiburg called from Los Angeles to say they were braving the storm, flying to Denver and would be up in the morning if they had to break through by dogsled. It also turned out to be midsemester college break, and we were suddenly besieged by wonderfully boisterous C.U. students.

"To think I just asked if we were expecting anyone," I whooped. "Can you believe this, Ken? Mother will think we have a full house, and the Linges are out of solitary confinement at last."

Friday's Winterskol Ball was a smash. We burrowed through the costume trunk to deck out our guests, and they had the time of their lives. Claytie went as Carmen Miranda, draped in bananas, salivating Chileans, and little else. I was Fanny Brice and Ken, Nicky Arnstein. Mrs. Packard had herself borne high on a Turkish rug-palleted platform as a plump, androgynous Merlin. She was beginning to believe her own and Claytie's publicity. She was levitated all right, by four visibly staggered high school football players.

Ellie made a pert leprechaun, and Jake clanked around in his drover's outfit wearing rackety, outsized spurs.

On Saturday morning, feeling a good deal less than hearty, Ken and I knuckled under to do the lodge chores. We were so queasy that it took our combined strength to totter through the work of one. Jake and Ellie fortunately had strong recuperative powers and were able somehow to get the horses harnessed, the hayrick hitched up, and everyone in place for the trek to the parade.

There was a blessed break in the snow although, as Freddie put it, it was "colder than a witch's tit." Harold Carr happily hammed it up in Freddie's bathtub, wrapped in blankets and clouds of smoke from buckets of dry ice and an enormous stogie. Ken, his head twice its normal size, was lugubriously enthroned, the Sears print blurring before his eyes. The Rices and the Grimes and the Linges were in bed with all the dogs. The children were in position, with Half-Whit adding a nice touch in his arm cast and a sign reading "Ski Bum." Annie and Mollie stamped, snorted and milled about, eager to roll and get warm.

The parade, like all parades, hemmed and hawed and backed and filled. The temperature dropped and all of us, except the children, consumed large quantities of the martinis Gerry Carr had thoughtfully provided in a gallon jug. By the time we got under way, Aspen's young crowd was ready for us with enormous pyramids of very icy ammunition, and most of the parade entrants were drunker than goats. The ensuing mayhem was awesome.

Harold Carr toppled out of the bathtub and into a snowbank on a curve. The children and Ken were pelted with unidentified flying objects, one of which cracked Fred Fisher's hallowed porcelain. "He'll beat me up," choked Ken. "And I'm not well." The Rices, Grimes, and Linges got under the quilts and stayed there, while the dogs all dove off to join the packs of gamboling hounds running amok through the streets.

The Chileans, along with many other Olympians on hand, managed to march smartly to an almost palpable skirl of bagpipes. They did not fall out and accept proffered drinks until we had staggered the final blocks toward the outskirts of town.

When we were called back to receive second prize, Ken mumbled ungraciously, "I suppose it's another useless trophy. Why don't they give out canned hams, I wonder?"

With the float emptied of people and dogs, Ellie collected our scattered remains in the station wagon, and we told Jake to gallop Annie and Mollie on back to the corral.

When Ken and I finally lurched out of the car gasping, "At last, a nap," we were greeted by Half-Whit, his lips blue with pain from the swelling inside his cast (he'd been throwing retaliatory snowballs), and Jake, waiting ashen-faced by the corral.

"My arm is killing me," Whit moaned. "It's Mollie, come quick," Jake cried. He added, "I called Doc Harlan, but he's off doctoring a sick herd and they don't know when he'll be back."

Ellie ran to administer to Whit, and Ken and I raced for Mollie's side. The poor old soul was prone on the ground, eyes wild, sides heaving, spittle drooling from her mouth.

"Baby," I cried, flinging myself on the snow beside her. "Oh Jake, she looks so sick."

"She started panting and stumbling right after we crossed the bridge. And we'd only trotted a couple of blocks," Jake said worriedly.

"I wonder if it's the heaves," Ken said.

"I thought you didn't know anything about horses."

"I don't."

"We'd better call Storrs. He does. And Jake, see if Buck Deane has any ideas until Doc Harlan gets here."

Storrs and Buck arrived and agreed that the important thing was to get Mollie on her feet.

"A sick horse must be kept upright," Storrs explained. "They are so heavy that they cut off their own circulation if they lie down too long."

Buck hurried off to T-Lazy-7 to get his truck with the winch and a canvas horse harness. When he returned it was after four o'clock, and Lee and Tiki John had arrived from the slopes in ice cream-colored Bogners, looking very unbucolic and offering a lot of inexpert council.

Getting a sixteen-hundred-pound horse who's incon-solable into a canvas winch and on her feet, in a corral soaked with new snow and turning into a quagmire from jostling, busy feet, is on a par with double arm wrestling a python and a crocodile. By the time poor bewildered Mollie was winched up and quivering on her tiptoes, Uris and Freiburg were silt-blackened to the thighs, McDuff had bitten Buck Deane, and the rest of us looked like losers at a mud pie throwing.

I ran around in circles calling to see if Doc Harlan was back from the cow pasture, checking the ice packs on Whit's cast, pouring drinks for our guests, helping Ellie register and settle in eight more college students, reinforcing Storrs and wondering fleetingly how I could have bemoaned the last few weeks as pallid.

Storrs, clearly as perplexed as though he'd never been closer to a horse than a brewery wagon, said, after downing some bourbon neat, "I think we'll have to keep lowering and raising her, make sure we aren't cutting off her breathing with that harness. It could be as risky as just letting her lie there."

"Oh, Storrs, you don't think she'll die?"

"She's in a pretty bad way."

Claytie tripped to the far fringes of the corral where, from a safe distance, she chirruped, "Never mind about the guests, lovey. I just got up, I'm fresh as a daisy, and Ellie and I have everything under control. Falling Rock and the boys will be over for a jam session soon. Don't forget this is the Chileans' last night. We're having a little impromptu celebration."

By nine o'clock that night Storrs, Buck, and Mollie were barely holding the line. Ken and I looked and felt like survivors of gladiatorial combat. The children and Ellie had cooked hot dogs for everyone doing veterinary duty and entertaining. Ulla Nillson, Rose Crumpacker, Elizabeth Chamberlain, Sheila DeVore, Mariellen Powers, and other friends were out from town. Bertie Cross, the artist, was on hand, as were the Norwegians, Lee, Tiki John, most of Stein's instructors, Arthur Langenkamp, and I forget who all. The Heatherbed was a seething cauldron.

Bugsy Barnard, our hip physician friend, stopped by and checked Whit's arm. He said doubtfully of Mollie, "I could give that horse a shot, man, but I can't think of a thing that would touch the Big Mother."

Falling Rock had recruited some of my kitchen pots for extra bongos, and "The Girl From Ipanema" was in full sway. Accompanied by The Cry, the Chileans, Claytie, and Jonathon Moore were leading a conga line of college students around the lounge, out the walkways, through the end suite, back outside, and into the lounge again. Large as that room was, it was absolutely thronged. To the already unsteady eye, it pounded, pulsated and throbbed. As I gulped down a hot dog, I wondered morbidly if double vision could become a permanent affliction.

Snow was again falling as dense as goose feathers, and Storrs and I had left Mollie long enough to grab a quick bite. Ken had succumbed completely. He was sound asleep in our big wing chair, clad in parade costume of red underwear, his mother's Spencer corset, and a bedraggled Minnie Pearl hat.

At 9:15 the Battle Cry had reached its zenith. Ruffy, Ike, and Damë had escaped the children and were in the lounge howling like Vladivostok wolves around a troika. There was a burst of terrible profanity and the sound of breaking crockery as Arnë Marthinsson tripped over a dog and fell into the gluehwein, spattering spiced burgundy over many virginal ski clothes. Fulminations in five languages were heard as drums pounded and dancers scattered. Then Bertie Cross sambaed too far in reverse and toppled into the wood bin with a splintering crash. At that moment the door was flung wide, and Uncle Whit reeled in with Mother at his heels.

Although attired smartly in mink and a pheasant hat in full plumage, Mother was decidedly the worse for wear. The mink was askew, the hat hanging crazily over one eye. She did not have her usual bandbox, ready-for-the-runway air.

Uncle Whit gave me a wild, haunted look and slumped into a handy chair. As music and dancing died a dissonant death, Mother bewilderedly surveyed the conga line, Ken in drag, Jonathon in a derby, Falling Rock in deerskins, and everyone covered in the grape or mud and gasped, "Is this what they call an orgy?"

For a moment I was too *hors de combat* to move. Then as the last Battle Cry echo died, one of the lovable Chileans filled a very awkward pause by crying, "Dohn tell us iss you so beyootiful mamacita?" With a low bow he swept her trembling glove to his lips.

"It's just old home week, mother," I said, managing a weary, very tentative hug. I was mud-spattered from head to toe. "And it really is nice to see you," I added weakly.

"You certainly didn't dress for it. You look as if you've been butchering."

Somehow everyone shifted gears and rushed into high to wait on mother—taking her coat, seating her by the crackling fire, plumping up cushions, removing her sodden shoes, carrying luggage, cleaning up wine dregs, fixing hot tea. Meanwhile I tried explaining (in order of their importance): the general bacchanalia; our Latin American and Norse delegations; the conga line and Battle Cry; one sick horse; one broken arm; Ken's informal attire; the upcoming Olympics; and my total lack of organization (with which she was already on intimate terms). It wasn't easy.

Mother said, "Just pour a little something stronger in this tea. Rum will do nicely, thank you. Let me unthaw a bit, and we'll take one thing at a time."

Uncle Whit confessed that he hadn't been the epitome of organization either. He'd made the two-hundred-and-twenty-five-mile trip from Denver so often he could fly it blind. His snappy little Austin-Healey got great speed and mileage. But, he said, he should have foreseen the inevitable—that the heaviest storm of the season would arrive chockablock with Mother. "I knew I should have traded that idiot's delight in on a four-wheel-drive truck. We were dredged out of ditches, pushed over mountains, rocked off a culvert by the State Police and towed twice," he fumed.

Poor Mother had spent hours standing in roadside drifts in her I. Miller pumps watching rescue operations. Her expression, to say nothing of her feet, had grown more frozen by the hour.

"Then we walked in on this scene of quiet domesticity," said Whit bitterly. "She'll never set foot in the state again . . . Oh, hi, Bugsy."

"Buck up, man," said Bugsy. "The kid's okay, the scene is grooving, it's only the horse that may be deadsville."

"Er, mother, this is Bugsy Barnard. We interned together."

"How's tricks, Mama?" asked Bugsy.

"I don't believe I caught your name," whispered Mother. She had the dazed look of a woman who wonders if her son served under an assumed name at St. Luke's Hospital for Advanced Entomology.

"They call me Bugs, Mrs. Whitcomb. I'm cool and far out. Always jiving."

For one frantic moment no one could remember Bugsy's baptismal name. "Er . . . Robert . . . Doctor ROBERT Barnard," Whit announced after delving deep into the recesses of his floundered mind.

"You're a physician?" Mother asked weakly, more than ever convinced she was in a charnel house or sink of sin.

"Well, I go the penicillin route, if that's what you mean, Mrs. W."

Whit shrugged resignedly. There was simply no way of cleaning up this scenario to Mother's strict specifications.

However, everyone not only kept rising, they positively soared to the occasion. Mother was soon not only thawed out but melting like a pat of braised butter. Jonathon managed to convey the impression that he'd leapt from the pages of Burke's Peerage. Ellie beguiled her with Irish blarney. Jake was a paradigm of willing servitude. John Rice and Scott Linge, more sedate medical men than Bugsy and a lot calmer than Whit, prescribed and supplied two hot water bottles and aspirin. Mrs. Packard had one of her rare streams of consciousness and not only ceased thrumming but to my open-mouthed astonishment confided chattily to Mother that she had attended Sophie Newcomb with one of her oldest and dearest friends. Sheila DeVore, who managed our bookstore and is as British as a brolly, and Mariellen Powers, California golden girl, turned on their considerable candlepower. Mother began to feel she was not a stranger in a strange land.

Finding her rosy-checked grandchildren tucked cozily in their beds helped.

"It hardly hurts at all," said Half-Whit, sleepily content in a small haze of Empirin and codeine.

"Well, I'm certainly not setting foot here in the winter again," mother assured the children. "I've seen what you poor darlings must endure. Why, it's a miracle you aren't all suffering frostbite."

"Just Mom," piped up Dan. "She has fwostbite on her chin." When the *Enfant Perdu* finally talked, he managed to say entirely too much.

"She has *what*?" Mother was horrified.

"It's just a little old spot left over from Mont Tremblant, Mother. Right out there on the Hapsburg family jaw," I said gaily. "I keep a scarf over my chin in cold weather so it won't give me trouble. But just wait until you see our bright, sunny days." I sent up an ardent prayer that one would arrive à la carte in the morning.

Having assured herself that Whit would not be crippled for life and that the rest of her progeny weren't frozen stiff in in their beds, Mother said, "Now, Martie, as soon as you find me a pair of serviceable boots and something warm besides mink, we'll go right on out to the corral for a look at that horse."

"But Mother . . ."

"Don't 'but' me, my dear. I grew up with horses, and I've forgotten more than you and Kenny will ever know."

Ken sighed and went to find boots, a heavy coat, and extra flashlights.

"Mother, you should climb straight into bed before you catch pneumonia."

"Not until we see to poor Mollie," said Mother firmly.

Later, with Storrs and Ken and I holding torches, Mother checked Mollie's heaving sides and lolling head. She questioned us about her exercise patterns. She looked in her mouth. At last she announced grimly, "I'm afraid this horse has Monday Morning Sickness."

"But it's only Saturday night," I exclaimed inanely.

"I believe the proper medical term is azoturia. Your grandfather always called it Monday Morning Sickness. It strikes old horses who haven't exercised and are subjected to sudden strains."

"What do we do for it?"

"The poor dear looks pretty far gone to me. It's usually fatal. You may have to shoot her."

"Oh, my God!"

Storrs said, his voice creaking, "She's twenty-five years old. I should have known better. I should have kept her right in the barn."

Later a weary Doc Harlan arrived, looked Mollie over, and said, "It's Monday Morning Sickness, and it's bad. Afraid we'll have to put her down."

"Isn't there anything we can do?" I pleaded, feeling like a trunk murderess.

"Not at her age."

While tears streamed down my cheeks, Mollie was dispatched to greener pastures in the sky. Ken could have said "I told you so," but he hitched up his corset, put an arm around me and walked me back to the lodge. "Doc tells me that horses are more fragile than dogs," he said reassuringly. "You mustn't blame yourself about Mollie."

"Y—you were right, Dad. From now on, I'll avoid horses like lepers."

"No you won't. Because we're going to have a great big string of them, and we're going to learn everything there is to know about them, too."

Ten years later we were nursing thirty-five horses and one hundred times as many headaches as the year we started.

*Book III
SURVIVAL
OF THE
FITTEST*

CHAPTER 13

Never Leave Honeymooners Alone

WE WERE making more discoveries about people than Margaret Mead among the Samoans. The most elemental was that you could not simply pass out drinks, fresh towels, and introductions and presto, have everyone fit right into the Sterling mold. It was Ken and I who were having to break out of old patterns and adjust.

Our guests covered the spectrum from Indians to cowboys; from Doc Wolfe, who pioneered radar, to Dr. Louise Tyrer, who invented the IUD; from spinach farmers to turkey breeders; from Gene Rayburn, TV host, to Vern Gagne, mastodon wrestler. We entertained Orientals who designed robots and played the viola; Jack Mormons who drank, smoked and caroused; and a few priests and plenty of Methodists who did likewise; the Neiman-Marcus and Lazarus department store families; physicists from Alamogordo and oceanographers from Woods Hole; skiers from Smackover, Arkansas, and Dimmitt, Texas; guests who skimped all year to pay for their vacations, and others who phoned the pilot and said, "Gas her up, Jim, we're flying to Aspen."

We also had a lot of nice normal people who moved calmly through their ski weeks having fun and doing nothing terribly exciting.

For Ken the first few years were hell. Weekly he faced a lounge packed with strangers, their faces as featureless as so many heads of cauliflower. Unless prompted by me, he referred to new guests as "You know, that oil driller with the hammy hands," or "No, the other single girl, the one from Springfield with the glasses," until he'd had time to sort and re-sort them like a tricky hand of gin.

As old guests returned (when I use the term "old" with our guests, it means they endured a lot in their yearly encounters with us, and it aged them), they became familiar faces and dearly beloved friends, and Ken was a happier man. In the interim, introductions were my job. If I do say it myself, I may have been a lunkhead with figures, but I was a whiz with names. I could ricochet around a roomful of fifty people like a cue ball, spieling off names and never missing a single Lorenzo Whitehead or Annie Lee Sokol.

We found that Canadians are marvelous people. You can warm your hands at their fires. This may have something to do with that cold climate they live in.

People from the West, we discovered, are easygoing, light-hearted, fun, and informal. So are people from New England and the mid-Atlantic states, although sometimes you must chip away a thin layer of veneer to get at the real them.

We were startled to find how often one man's poison is another man's meat.

Anne and Al Brown were a darling older couple who arrived from Kansas City our first February and annually thereafter so that Anne could rest and read, and Al could repair the lodge. He was in nirvana unscrewing every faucet in the place, soaking off lime deposits (our water was harder than Bethlehem steel) and replacing them shining like Reed & Barton flatware. After the fixtures were polished, the plumbing was in apple pie order, the doors all trued up and closing like spring zephyrs, Al found out about the wood cutting. After that he arrived twice a year, first making certain that Ken had his woodlots lined up and ready for demolition. Al was not happy until they had laid in ten full cords of aspen, spruce, and scrub oak, and Ken's eyes were as glazed as jelly doughnuts. I was always a little disappointed he didn't offer to turn out new draperies for all the windows.

We learned that the altitude could be injurious to our guests' health.

People simply could not leave Milwaukee, drive straight through to Aspen, hurtle up and down our eleven-thousand-foot mountains, guzzle pitchers of martinis and expect to feel reborn. It takes three full weeks to acclimatize to high altitudes, and very few of our guests had that kind of time. At the risk of being great big bores, we cautioned them morning, noon, and night about moderation in eating, skiing, and drinking. Especially drinking. A four-highball man at sea level was liable to have his first hallucinogenic experience after two Scotches in rarified air.

Living in a house party hotel, the children grew enormously blasé about "drunk and disorderly" in its many manifestations. Not that they were surrounded by lushes, but they did witness a lot of very nice people temporarily out of order.

One Sunday evening deep into our weekly get-acquainted party, I was rushing down the front steps for more ice when I heard voices from what, come summer, would be a large iris bed above a three-foot stone wall.

"You fink, Mike, I told you to hang onto his other foot."

"I tried, Whit, but he's awful big and floppy."

"Well, straddle his leg, stupid. You and I can pull while the girls steer his head and hold up his arms."

I peeked around the corner to find our five oldest heaving and tugging at a very large, thoroughly soused guest spraddled in the snow.

"He's snoring," Mike snorted. "Right out here in this freezing weather. Man, is he tanked."

"At least he isn't dead," puffed DearGwen.

"Name's Torino. Whash yours, honey," said the drunk, his mouth muffled in cotton.

"If we drag him into that bunkroom, maybe we can sober him up under the cold water."

"Waaaaattteeerrrr boy!" sang Mr. Torino.

"Just so I don't have to undress the spazz," Dede muttered.

Mr. Torino segued into the first three bars of "Melancholy Baby."

"Who says we have to? We'll just get him to the can and stick his head in the shower," Mike said matter-of-factly.

"Aprriiiiil Shoooooooooooweeeeeeers," howled Mr. Torino.

"I'm not sure he's worth saving," sniffed Whit.

"He's a guest of Mom's and Dad's, commodehead. And mom's got enough on her hands without this three-hundred-pound klutz."

By this time the children had edged Mr. Torino to the bunkroom door and were practically home. They were managing so well that I tiptoed on down the stairway, leaving them to their mountain rescue. After all, a few repulsive drunks at this formative stage could only serve as memorable nonrole models for their later years.

There were some truisms we discovered but never fully understood. For example, All Psychiatrists' Children Are Monsters.

Listen, this is exactly the kind of blanket statement made by boors and bigots, and I know that I should be saying good things about all people. But we honestly never housed one psychiatrist who wasn't destructively permissive with his or her offspring.

Our initial psychiatric couple were a bright, rather hirsute pair from somewhere south of the Jersey Flats. They talked a lot about subliminal urges, repressed aggressions,

144

and the purity of young minds and wore heavy thong sandals and Peruvian serapes après-ski. They had removed their children, aged five and eight, from school and transported them to Aspen for the "learning experience." While the rest of us learned more about castration fears and erogenous zones than we really cared to know, the Jersey kids learned by tearing our lounge limb from limb, pouring breakfast orange juice in the coffee urn and using blueberry muffins for impromptu games of volleyball.

Then one afternoon Robin and Gwendy rushed into the kitchen with Danny, albino blue and quivering, wrapped in their parkas.

"He was running down the driveway in his birthday suit," Gwen said tearfully.

"We're going to kill the kid who did it."

"Did what?" I yelled frantically as I hugged the infant, pummeling him like a Swedish masseuse. "Oh, darling baby boy, what were you *doing*?" I cried. While Ellie held a frenzied long-distance conference with Uncle Whit about lowered body temperatures, the girls and I thumped Dan until his teeth rattled like shell corn in a bowl. Eventually we pounded him back to his normal rosy color and immersed him in a warm tub, although he felt clammier than a crayfish for hours.

The elder Jersey kid may only have been eight, but his Machiavellian mind was that of a sixty-year-old. He had paid Dan fifty dollars to run around the lodge bare-bottomed. Furthermore, he paid him in Monopoly money, which he apparently kept handy for just such underaged patsies. The *Enfant Perdu* proudly displayed his loot to his sisters, explaining that he planned to buy me a valentine. I nearly went to pieces.

When I regained my composure, I confronted Machiavelli's parents with their child's act of malfeasance. They smiled fondly at the little dear as the father stated, "We like to indulge our children's sense of original thought."

With all my heart I yearned to administer a good strong

clout to the grinning Original Thinker.

The psychiatrists' spawn we knew may have grown into well-adjusted adults, but in their formative years they all majored in espionage and Pol Pot mind control.

Among other Interesting Facts On All-Time File was that no lodge is complete without its in-house grouser. It helps blow off everyone's steam.

We first met our own grouser when Mike came in from school one day and announced, "There's a man in the furnace room who says he's testing the pressure gauge. But he's wearing neat city clothes, he looks like a college guy, and he has a drink in his hand."

I raced hell-for-leather to see if we might have a Weatherman about to wire the place for stick bombs and ran headlong into Dick McKaughan, president of Texas International Airlines and nitpicker to the Western World. "I think your pressure's too high," he said. "Want a shot of Scotch?"

With his unlimited supply of free air travel, Dick appeared at frequent intervals to inquire loudly how much we charged for a room with heat; what sacrificial offerings were required to obtain hot water; why was the coffee never ready at six o'clock in the morning, ad infinitum. On those rare occasions when all was in perfect working order, he suffered a terrible setback and it ruined the trip for him. No season would have reached true low ebb without McKaughan carping in the background. We adored the man.

Above all, we learned, never leave honeymooners alone.

Midway through the season we were joined by a dewy-eyed, hand-holding couple who'd been married in a gala hometown ceremony only a few days before. They hadn't been with us thirty-six hours when Ken said to me at lunch, "Martie, I think our newlyweds are having problems. The bride seems out of sorts."

"Out of sorts?" I squealed. "Those two are busier than finches hunting a tree to nest in. When I try to introduce them or mention 'honeymoon,' Cindy blushes the colors of a Mexican sunset, and Rob chokes up like a grade-school debater."

"Well, if you don't believe me, why is that child in her room crying?"

I cantered right up to room six, knocked and found our first bride indeed as tear streaked as Melinda on the Moors.

"Why, Cindy dear, whatever is the matter?" I asked, taking her in my well-seasoned, motherly arms.

"I—I'm not sure," she sniffled, honking into her hand-kerchief.

"Well, let's have a nice long chat and find out. Where's Rob?"

"Out skiing. Alone. The rat."

Uh, oh, I thought. Unfond memories of Mont Tremblant welled up.

After I'd reheated the coffee and we'd talked things through, I discovered that the bride was as bereft as a housewife deprived of her soaps. Like me, she'd been dragged from the bosom of her family by a big brute who kept skiing off and leaving her to sink or snowplow. Unlike me, she was about as athletic as a lace doily. She abhorred skiing, and she wasn't very happy with her brand new husband.

In those days it was not yet *de rigueur* to live together before marriage, and the sudden jolt of sharing shower, bed, days, and nights with a big hairy stranger could be traumatic for a girl. Coupled with the demands of some very large ski mountains, it was enough to lead to ana-phylactic shock.

Well, after I'd regaled her with tales of my own nuptial pain and suffering, Cindy giggled into her damp hankie and decided she wasn't cut out to play Emma Bovary. She settled instead for lunching with my younger friends, shopping in Aspen's lovely boutiques and charging some darling new clothes to her unwitting spouse. "That'll get his attention," I promised her.

As for us, we practically strong-armed Cindy and Rob into the center of attention. I won't say that we got into bed with them, but we did keep them surrounded and occupied. Rob grew so grateful for the times they were alone that he even stayed off the mountain long enough to take his wife to a hospital benefit luncheon.

We never again treated honeymooners as if they were on religious retreat.

CHAPTER 14

The Ski Instructor

"OH, THERE'S something about a parka," I sang playfully as Ken preened in front of our bedroom mirror in his instructor's uniform.

"Dammit, cut that out," he roared. Getting ready for troop inspection was demanding enough without an irreverent wife peering over his shoulder.

Every morning Stein inspected his instructors like a Marine Corps general conducting full dress review. Turtlenecks were to be immaculate and designated colors only; hair neatly trimmed; ski boots (pre-Bakelite) shined to a Hepplewhite glow. An instructor out of line, step, or sorts was a man out of a job.

Oh, I'll admit those early Eriksen forces were a thing of beauty, especially in the famed Stein sweater. Stein's delightful mother hand-knit the originals, tastefully and warmly designed in the ski school colors of black and red. They somehow made the shoulders straighten, chests jut out, alpenhorns sound. Those sweaters were something you lived up to.

In January when one of the older Vikings got drunker than a lord during a Sun Valley race weekend, Stein stood him in front of the troops and stripped him of his sweater and all his ski school patches. We felt it was no less than he deserved.

Despite being the center of all eyes and a lot of undeserved attention, the ski instructor of our day led a life of quiet desperation. When not being pinched, pursued and mooned over by rapacious divorcées, his greatest preoccupation was survival. By survival I do not mean the physical hazards of the ski mountain. I am talking about the weekly grocery bill.

Timmy Hayden was tall, devilishly attractive, and a wonderful instructor. While teaching at the Highlands, he reared a passel of lovely children; built Lynne's and his house with his own clever hands; and shot, trapped, or fished for all of the family meat. He and Lynne slept in a bed so cramped that Tim's long legs were propped nightly on their freezer chest. This saved space and also served as a makeshift protection system for their precious frozen food supply. The Haydens existed almost exclusively on venison, elk, trout, and wild duck, and Timmy ate such a regular diet of fish sandwiches for lunch that we expected him to break out in speckles like a Dolly Varden trout. (To this day, I cannot face a row of glassy fish eyes in a freezer without thinking of Tim and shuddering.)

When Teddy Armstrong took Mary to wife, Mary's mother was appalled to learn that her tenderly reared daughter had married a ski instructor. In a frantic telephone call to Aspen she inquired, "But how much is Theodore making a week, Mary?" Mary called into the other room, "Teddy, Mother wants to know how much you're making."

"Tell the old broad thirty dollars a week and all the snow we can eat," growled Teddy. After teaching all day, filling in as maître d' at the Onion and playing drums in the Limelight's after-dinner combo, Teddy was a little cranky.

I have watched him pound his way through an entire solo riff while sound asleep in his chair.

Far above Ted and Timmy on an exalted plateau by themselves were the skiing greats: Freidl Pfeiffer, Christian Pravda, Fred Iselin, Stein Eriksen, Anderl Molterer. These were the medal winners, the Olympians, the living legends. Younger instructors moved worshipfully around their parameters, awestruck and circling from a distance.

Not Ken. At thirty-six, his innate irreverence was entrenched for life. He had no known neuroses, a love of the ludicrous, and a hell of a lot of self-esteem. During Sunday demonstrations Stein would announce to the large viewing audience, "Und now Kenny Sterling will illustrate his werry graceful vedeln turns," only to have Ken career crazily down the hill, bowing and gesticulating maniacally to the crowd. Just as Stein was addressing one of his classes in stentorian Norse accents, Ken would leap gleefully for an overhead branch and smother him in snow, or ski over the backs of his skis to despoil his golden image. It goes without saying that Stein was a "schwell shport."

The Stein Eriksen Winter Carnival featured Ken, Timmy Hayden, and Ted Armstrong as head clowns. At first the younger Vikings were puzzled and confused by the Americans' ribald humor and apparent disrespect for authority. They had been reared to stand at attention before one's leaders, and it was hard for them to go against this early training. But slowly, by easy stages, they got into the act. They performed acrobatics on chair lifts, leaped off into the trees, kissed the girls and even joked (albeit shakily) with Stein.

They were learning the Yankee tenet that a smile can be your umbrella. It dawned on them that the caring instructors were practicing every trick short of human sacrifice to dupe their ski school students into leaning *down* that formidable mountain instead of *up*; chivvying them into holding those chattering skis parallel; and coaxing them into eventual excellence. Although skiing still required great grit, Ken and Teddy and Timmy did their darnedest to bewitch their beginners into thinking they were enrolled in the Comedy Store instead of the School of Basic Skiing and Hard Knocks.

The boys also did their best to lighten Stein's load.

One of the prices Stein paid for fame (and there were plenty) was the private lesson. For twenty dollars—the equivalent of one hundred and fifty dollars today—an hour, anyone under the sun could buy Stein's time and purchase his hard-pressed soul.

A rather well-known fashion designer once signed on for a week of private lessons and her cut of the Eriksen pie. Daily she rode the chair with "our leader" and pinched, patted and stroked that famous fanny until Stein was red-faced and stammering. From morning until night the Terrible Threesome let Stein know they were thinking of him. Ken greeted him around the hill with lusty choruses of "My Time Is Your Time"; Teddy sang, "Did You Ever See A Stein Walking?"; and Timmy hummed, "For He's A Jolly Good Squeeze-Oh." At the end of the week Stein slunk off to Winter Park to lick his wounds.

There were times of course when this instructor worship got decidedly out of hand. Especially when some of our women guests made perfect fools of themselves over a man we knew to be just slightly brighter than the village idiot. But there was something mystical about those uniforms. Even in today's age of ERA enlightenment, I know females who still go all gaga over a guy in a ski school suit. He may have bad breath and scoliosis, but if he sports a dark tan and that parka *distinguè* he has only to bark, "Jump!" and some fool woman will squeak, "How high?" I did it myself. Remember André of the Laurentians?

Despite lots of shenanigans, ski school progressed at a more or less predictable pace. The slowest day of the week was always Saturday. This was the busy time at the lodges when old guests departed, a clean broom made way for the new, and the innkeeper's wife collapsed over her fallen arches. Meanwhile, the ski schools were sunk in a morass of gloom. Sundays were not much better. Sunday was the time newcomers wobbled about testing their ski legs and meeting the mountain. Ah, but Monday. Monday was the banner day at ski school. Hundreds of hopefuls, their eyes shining with anticipatory zeal, signed up for instruction.

Any tyro could start Monday with a full class. The trick was to keep those students coming for the entire week. Sought after by every ski instructor, week's end was as elusive and desirable as a perfect attendance pin for Sunday school.

Once Ted, Timmy, Ken, and cohorts had their classes on the dotted line, they employed every wile in their repertoires to reach Friday with a full roster. They dangled lavish wine picnics—for which the thoroughly gulled women students usually furnished the repast—like carrots on sticks labeled "Friday." And they constantly extolled the ski school merit badge (awarded only at the Friday afternoon cocktail party) despite its being an ugly little creation forged of base metal. That first year Magnë and Arnë watched in consternation when their students slipped out of their hands like sand through a sieve. But they learned fast. Their glib patter and tricks of the trade improved in direct proportion to their desire to eat and pay the rent.

Like every other novice, Ken started at the bottom. The bottom, in ski parlance, was the Banana Belt. Here politics ran rampant. A Banana Belter who'd been working miracles with his class for days would suddenly find everyone yanked out from under him and passed along to a senior instructor—one who'd lost his own students the minute business slacked off after midweek. Many Banana Belters grew despondent, to say nothing of their pupils, who by this time adored the snow the man trod and were averse to starting over again with new loyalties. However, the hell with the students. Seniority was all. (I don't know if this is still being done, but I should hope not.)

Because Ken was un-neurotic, he never remained unemployed for long. Stein's *oberlieutenants* fobbed all their problem skiers off on this willing worker.

Claytie, true to her promise, appeared for ski school looking alarmingly unathletic in graduated shades of blue. She announced loudly to Stein, "I'll have Father Sterling as my instructor, please."

There was snickering in the ranks. Stein said, "We assign instructors according to the student's abilities."

"Very well then, I'll have Father for private lessons."

Ken, blushing crimson, felt as if he were being "had" over coffee and cognac like a piece of brie.

Claytie paid for but did not partake of a series of expensive private lessons that would have gladdened the heart of an Arthur Murray dance instructor. Ken did not feel a bit guilty when she grew bored and begged off due to ill health, weak knees, or late nights. "Her karma and her body are in terrible shape," he said, shuddering deeply and looking heavenward toward his Maker. Even Father had his limits.

The Banana Belter's existence was akin to life on an assembly line. Seasoned oldsters taught all the things that were fun—stem christies, parallel turns, racing, and deep powder classes—their worn and faded parkas darting atmospherically around the tops of the mountains and expert trails. Down at the bottom, in the Sink of Despair, drawing first blood on the T-bar and Half-Inch lifts, were the bright, shiny parkas of the new instructors. Toward the end of the first season even sunny Ken was growing choleric about his work.

"I don't even have to ski well, for God's sake," he snarled at his wife and children. "It's beyond me why I passed all those brute-strength, high-skill tests in Instructor's Clinic. I haven't done a thing but snowplow ever since."

"But you have a really neat tan," said Dede, anxious to please.

"And wonderful muscles," said DearGwen.

"The sacrifices I make to keep this family in food and ski wax," moaned the Banana Belter, wallowing in the attention and staggering in the direction of his easy chair. Admittedly he had the gait of a Marlboro cowboy and the gnarled back of a Cro-Magnon man. The snowplow was still doing terrible things to people. (I am pleased to report that the snowplow has finally "passed over," albeit not before thousands of hapless skiers have become spavined for life.)

Fortunately the short ski emerged to save an entire generation of incipient arthritics. Thanks to this wondrous invention, coupled with the passing of the snowplow, people today learn to ski in weeks instead of years. They master turns, high speeds, and mogul hopping at court-reporter speed. The Banana Belt is still there, but its scope is greatly diminished. It wasn't a minute too soon.

In those "olden days," (as the children still refer to them while Ken and I brush the crumbs from our Rough Rider uniforms), ski schools boasted anywhere from twelve to twenty instructors instead of two or three hundred. Every ski school was a tight little island, its instructors banded together against the world and the competition.

Magnë and Arnë, having shared beginner's English, ship's steerage, and many Red Onion Specials, were at first loathe to trust anyone but each other. Left to themselves, they got into some awesome jams. When they purchased their first fifty-dollar car without advice of attorney or driver's education, they promptly banked it off the Thunderbowl, went careening across Mrs. Paepcke's ranch, splintered blocks of downtown fences, bounced off the ticket booth of the Isis Theatre and came to rest just short of the hospital emergency room. "Ay couldn't find de damgotten stopper," howled Arnë in disgust.

The peculiar American practice of purchasing health and accident insurance—just one more inane custom to boys from a socialist monarchical republic with free medical care—struck them as something else they could live without.

"I'll lend you the thirty dollars for your premiums," Stein said. "Just be sure you apply immediately. Everyone in ski school must have accident insurance."

When Stein's back was turned, the boys talked it over and Arnë concluded, "Dis INsurance cost too damgotten much." Magnë nodded his head in agreement, and they went off to Stein's shop to pick out their new ski equipment. There they ran headlong into another odd Americanism, the Head ski. Howard Head had recently revolutionized the sport with his invention of a multilayered, high-tech, laminated ski that had many variations of spring, weight, and musical tone, plus soft, medium, and hard cambers. In Norway the boys had skied on a slightly improved version of the cumbersome twelve-foot hickories worn by Snowshoe Thompsen in the mid-19th century. Blithely out of date, Magnë and Arnë selected Head skis in the racing class and went up the mountain to strut their stuff. Within an hour they were back.

Expert skiers, they had suffered the multiple indignities of pratfalls, somersaults, and eggbeaters. At first they thought there was some awful unmagical quality about Colorado snow. Then Teddy took pity on them and explained the gyroscopic performance of the new Head. Nevertheless, it had been years since either of them so much as teetered on a pair of skis, and it struck fear into their young hearts. Arnë said, "Magnë, already I'm taking oudt dat damgotten INsurance vrom Stane."

"Arnë, I take him tew. Bedder ve starve den break de heads."

They nearly did, those first few weeks. Starve, that is.

Their insurance payments left them, we found out later, with thirty-two dollars to see them through their first month in this country. During this initiation period their breakfast was tea fortified with quantities of sugar and replenished with hot water. (They carried their own tea bag, which often saw service for days.) Lunch was crackers and hot water, sometimes spiced with catsup or mustard. The crackers swelled up and gave them a nice full feeling.

Their students sometimes bought them lunch, but not often. Unlike Ken and his fellow connivers, the Vikings were not yet smooth talkers and far too ingenuous to deliberately con anyone out of a meal. Their unwitting pupils, many of them richer than Croesus, could have afforded it. But they looked on these shy young Norwegians as *ski instructors*, Eddic figures from Norse drama, above supping with mere snowplow peasantry. If they'd only known the poor kids were faint from hunger.

In the close quarters we inhabited, you can see why I lost any awe of ski instructors I might have harbored from my youth.

What I found most admirable about the instructor was his dogged devotion to duty. To me his greatest achievement was just appearing at ski school on a daily basis. Especially when it was ten below zero, the wind was howling like a depraved Laplander, and the mountain was lost in funnels of whiteout. I myself am psychologically unable to leave a warm fireside for a cold chairlift at 8:30 in the morning. I am unable to leave for anywhere at all at 8:30 in the morning, and my heart swelled with pride as my manful spouse strode up the snow and windswept driveway, his long, purposeful legs carrying him straight into the next Ice Age.

Even in Aspen we have our cold snaps. And due to circumstances beyond my control, I have occasionally been on hand for a ski school clinic on a bitter cold day at 10:00 A.M. There I have watched in horror as bare-handed instructors checked each student's bindings, adjusted boots, cleaned packed snow from skis, and stalwartly attended their frozen, immobilized charges. In those Rough Rider days there were no down mittens, no down-filled parkas, no insulated ski boots, or toasty warm-up suits. Even Iglook suffered his share of frostbite. No wonder ski instructors develop skin as brown and cured as pemmican. It's their homegrown carapace against the elements.

Like every instructor's wife, I sometimes grew irate over the harsh conditions, uncertain salaries, and brutish, boring work.

"What do you mean, you spent the morning stringing telephone lines?" I demanded of Ken.

"Well, there were only two classes, and they like to keep us busy."

"For how much an hour?" I sneered.

"Now, Martie, you know we're expected to pitch in with repairs and —"

"—and Sunday demos and instructor's clinics and about three hundred other volunteer jobs," I carped. "I'm surprised no one's asked you to shine Stein's boots.

"And furthermore," I was shouting by this time, "half of those striplings over there are barely surviving."

"Everyone's in the same boat," Ken sighed, "even Stein. All of us just have to work three jobs until things get better."

One evening when half the ski school was huddled over martinis in our kitchen, I finally pounded the table and thundered, "Let's strike."

"You mean picket lines at the T-bar?" Gene Clausen asked quizzically.

"They tried forming a union on Aspen Mountain, and you know what happened. The organizers were fired," Peder Klyve said dejectedly.

"We're not union types anyhow," Teddy said. "We're free spirits, baby."

"Don't ever forget," said Timmy Hayden, "that there are more and more ski-mad jerks gathering in the trenches every day. All waiting in line to take over my parka."

"Vot is dat strike?" asked Arnë perplexedly.

I gave up.

Well, the important thing was for the public to learn skiing as painlessly and prettily as possible. Once they did, they would be privy to the nearest thing to flying that we mortals can achieve on feet of clay. Helping mankind throw off his tiresome coil and reach this apogee was certainly heady stuff. It seemed to me that the good instructors felt something of the crusader's exaltation.

Our plumed knight may have appeared heroic and all-conquering to the outside world. Inwardly he was a man seething with domestic concerns. A man who trudged wearily home to a hectic hotel. Whose nagging wife suspected there was something immoral about skiing for a living and that he'd been up on that mountain munching bonbons, drinking sherry and having fun all day. Despite frostbitten fingers and a pinched expression, poor Ken could never quite disabuse me of this obsession. Not even when he changed into old clothes, shoveled the walks and suffered acid indigestion from too many lunch hour knockwursts and Oh Henry bars eaten on the run. Not even when he fought off waves of flatulence, bolted down his dinner and disconsolately dragged himself off to a required evening meeting on first aid or avalanche control.

Simply because he appeared all trim and tailored on ski school mornings, white teeth glistening in sun-blackened face, his six feet *soigné* in sleek Bogners, the parka slung rakishly over one shoulder, was no reason, no reason at all, for me to catch my breath, act the twittering school girl and embrace him passionately in front of all those children.

CHAPTER 15

The Racer's Edge

WHILE THEIR father labored in the instructor corps, our children went in hot pursuit of ski trophies and meniscus surgery. All those nights, weekends, holidays, after-school, and mother's days were producing results and taking their toll. Already Mike and Whit had progressed from Simple Simon kiddies' races to competing in, and winning, four-way meets. They had also embarked on what would be a series of thirty-eight family fractures. Before we were done, every orthopedist in town was driving a new car purchased with our hard-won money.

The four-way meet was a barbarous exercise in which a child ran a tricky slalom course, followed by an exhausting giant slalom. After drawing a shuddering breath, he skied cross-country dodging stumps and mine shafts and finally clamped on a set of jumpers to soar off sixty-meter hills. All of this required not only agility and diversity on the part of the child, but also steel nerves and a lot of sleight of hand regarding equipment from the mother.

"You can't be serious," I said to Half-Whit in disbelief when he announced for the first of what would be endless times, "Mom, I have to have another pair of skis."

"You already have a pair of skis," I said exasperatedly, "those Spaldings that exacted my last pound of flesh."

"But those are slaloms, Mom. I need a pair of G.S.'s too." Whit's eyes were wide as he added, "Now that I'm gonna travel with the team, you want me to win, don't you?"

I wasn't so all-fired sure. Not at those prices. It was bad enough that every last child would outgrow skis, boots, poles, parkas, and pants in the normal course of a year. The prospect of multiple sets of everything per customer filled me with icy foreboding.

"All I had in mind for them was plenty of fresh air and exercise," I wailed to their father. "I don't have the least idea how to whip up a breakfast for champions." Then I added darkly, "And don't you think that boy is awfully young to be traveling with those great big high school racers?"

"But mom, coach says I'm good."

"Good for what?" inquired his father.

"Aw, Dad, cut that out."

No one could accuse *us* of being skating mothers.

Not only did we have to come up with enough equipment to supply the Tenth Mountain Division, it soon developed that I was expected to do my duty as chauffeur/chaperone. I said dejectedly to Half-Whit's other parent, "They're only inviting me because I have a gas credit card, and they know a sucker when they see one."

"He's your child. It is our duty to foster wholesome competition among the young. And I have taken my turn," said the hard-hearted father callously. He had escorted a group of killer kids to Colorado Springs only the week before. They had kept him awake most of one night, and Guido Meyer Jr. had thrown up over the velvety interior of Lee Uris's brand-new Chrysler. Ken is well-known for his early-bird hours, weak stomach, and dislike of explaining things like the strong smell of naptha to a bosom buddy who's loaned him a vehicle. He wasn't volunteering for more race duty than he had to.

"But what do I say to great big boys who shave and use jock straps and know the facts of life!" I cried.

"Teach them all twelve verses of 'Roll Me Over' and they'll be yours forever," Ken said unhelpfully.

"I just don't think I'm cut out to be a racer chaser."

"You were born to it, Martie, you might as well face the music." (Over the next ten years I figure I logged sixty thousand miles, chased four hundred and eighty junior racers and faced more music than Beethoven, Bach, and Brahms.)

I am happy to report that at least mountain driving no longer dismayed me. I had braved enough blizzards, slides, and Loveland and Vail passages so that I now felt quali- fied to tackle the Klondike. My acrophobia was like a case of arrested TB—still there, but blessedly dormant.

My first trip as chaperone, up the Yampa Valley to Steamboat Springs, sounded pleasant enough. Parents new to the circuit were lured into the race trap with ini- tially easy trips. Before they knew what was happening, they found themselves in Ruidoso on the Mexican border one weekend and forging into the Grand Tetons the next. Junior racers had itineraries that would have made Thor Heyerdahl blanch, and we Westerners thought nothing of driving sixteen hundred miles for a three-day ski meet. Nowadays parents uncork a bottle of wine by the fire while their youngsters flick through commuter books, then catch the next plane. In the Rough Rider days the closest thing to a commuter airline was an occasional griz- zled bush pilot. Back then we parents battled washboard roads, avalanche detours, and gritty eyes and counted ourselves lucky if we had four-wheel drives.

Reluctantly, but at last, I started the drive to Steamboat on a snowy Thursday afternoon. Mine was one of three carloads of racers aged nine to eighteen, with three or four sets of skis per racer. Since the Heatherbed had an oversized ski rack, the top of our wagon groaned under the weight of seventeen pairs of skis and poles. Inside, the car pulsated with the burping and farting of small boys in devil red parkas and demonic expressions, preparing themselves for the heat of ski battle.

Ken's final instructions to me were, "Don't forget, if you hit a patch of ice, pump the brakes and turn into your skid."

"Pump the brakes and turn into the skid, pump the brakes and turn into the skid," I hummed to myself in the interludes between refereeing digestive scrimmages. At 8:30 that evening as we rounded a sheer rock face, I was still unconsciously mumbling, "Pump your brakes and turn . . ." when we struck a sheet of glare ice and slithered toward what looked like the La Brea Tar Pits immediately on our right.

"Everybody hit the floor," I shouted, pumping the brakes and turning into the skid. As we careened toward the pits, I had a split second to question Iglook's mental health and driving instructions before the car swerved abruptly and headed back toward the sheer rock face. Fortunately things happened in slow motion, and I had just time to steer the front wheel into a deep ditch at the foot of the sandstone wall. This braked us to a jouncing crawl. But as we bounced, seventeen pairs of skis and poles shot off the rack directly into the path of the car.

In a hairbreadth decision of which I've always been proud, I turned the car head-on into the sandstone to avoid crunching piles of precious equipment. The damage to the wagon was roughly equivalent to a month's hotel profits, but those skis had been purchased with whole families' sweat and sacrifice.

A cadre of shaken boys clambered out and one shouted, "Boy, Mrs. Sterling, it drops off about a thousand feet over here."

"Man, you sure saved all our skis and poles. Hardly even a scratch."

"How about our necks, you guys? Let's hear it for Mrs. Sterling."

Blushing prettily in the starlight, I knew how the Gipper felt when he won one for Notre Dame.

When we clanked into Steamboat Springs, the boys had abandoned burping and farting and were belting out "Onward Christian Soldiers."

The other chaperones were a distraught new father champing to get home to the maternity ward, and one of those mothers who wore Earth shoes, white ankle socks, and a prim expression of Christian forebearance. I went to bed that night without so much as a jigger of gin. I was black and blue from rebounding off the steering wheel. And I am not happy reading by a bare light bulb suspended from the ceiling. Furthermore, I detest bath towels the size and consistency of Scott paper products. I was now a hotel proprietor, and I had my standards.

After that first trip I knew enough to carry extra blankets and pillows, a reading lamp, sleeping bag, beach towels, a portable bar, and other bare necessities for subsistence-level living at large. However, I never flaunted these appurtenances in front of motel or hotel owners. I was learning early that I must get on their good side and stay there at all costs. In those days it required the witchery of Vestal Virgins to talk our way back into half the hotels in the Rocky Mountains. One year the Aspen Junior Ski Team was unable to obtain accommodations closer than seventy-five miles to several pivotal race finals.

Neophyte that I was, I had assumed that gate running, ski jumping, and cross-country racing would leave our junior achievers panting for the sack by seven o'clock nightly. *Au contraire.* I would like to state here and now that excesses of activity only serve to wind small skiers up to a state approaching jet propulsion. By nightfall ours were so hyperactive they were jamming up vending machines; giving the smaller kids whirlies in the toilets; using room walls for basketball backboards; coating every toilet seat in sight with Sloan's Liniment; and soaking their bed sheets in water, hanging them out the windows to freeze, then breaking them into thousands of splintery shards. One small boy asked me anxiously, "Mrs. Sterling, do we have to pay for frostbited sheets?"

Yes, we did have to pay for "frostbited" sheets. Also fractured machines, punched-out walls, cracked porcelain, and anything else the proprietor could locate with a fine-tooth comb.

CHAPTER 16

The Heatherbed Edge

IT IS MY theory that we in Colorado turn out champion skiers, climbers, and adventurers because we live up here on top of the world in constant danger of slipping off. The black chasm of the Yampa was only one of thousands on every side, and we who'd elected to settle dead center in one of the world's most treacherous mountain chains had to face facts. Our lives, like our children's, would be spent on the racer's edge.

Because the Heatherbed was situated spang at the foot of the Highlands ski mountain, and at the bottom of a steep driveway overhanging Maroon Creek tumbling along one hundred feet below, our location made for many sensational views. But I cannot say too little about the safety factor. The time was approaching when we would feel like a St. Bernard hospice hanging by tooth and toenail between here and eternity. Ellie's heartfelt hope never to see another basket case would prove in vain. She was about to become the resident nurse for a wayside aid station serving the purlieus of West Aspen and all of its environs.

One evening not long after my Steamboat excursion, as Ken was driving Gwendy and Dee home from their piano lessons through a driving snowstorm, he dimly spotted what appeared to be fresh tire tracks disappearing over the yawning void skirting the entrance to our driveway. For a moment he experienced that sense of unreality one feels looking at a cartoon with ski tracks dividing on each side of a tree, then coming together again.

When he jumped out, peered into the Black Hole of Calcutta and hallooed, he got no answer. But he thought he detected a faint light about sixty feet below.

"Do you girls see anything?" he asked anxiously.

"My hands are over my eyes," said Dede.

"Someone with a flashlight is down in that big hole, Daddy," Gwen said.

"That does it. Stand guard, girls!" and Ken scuttled off to our guest lounge.

"Call the sheriff, Martie. I need a hand, Jake. In fact, I need all hands. Everybody up, someone's over the side." Then Ken made the never-to-be-forgotten error of bawling, "Better bring some towels."

Our skiers were deep in that lavender hour when all is gin, vermouth, and euphoria, but they dumped their drinks in the potted plants and moved faster than women on their way to a white sale.

As Ken backed our big cattle truck to the edge of the black hole and lowered a heavy tow rope, some thirty guests stood clustered like a battery of wine stewards, towels draped over every arm and shoulder. They had, we learned later, gathered all the clean sheets and towels from their bedrooms *and* the linen supply closet.

Since Jake was young, brawny, and a veteran of many mock amphibious assaults, he was assigned the first sortie downward. After scaling the escarpment like a mountain goat, he clambered back doubled over and gulping for air.

"It's a cab!" he gasped. "Six people . . . mostly conscious . . . the cab driver's disappeared . . . one woman's in pretty bad shape . . . jeez, were they glad to see me."

Jake had located the wayward cab wedged upside down against a large Engelmann spruce in about eight feet of snow. It seemed the cab driver, looking for the Hindquarter Restaurant in the storm, had missed his turn, backed around and dropped off on his way to infinity. What Ken and Gwendy had seen was the ceiling light, the only auto part apparently still functioning. No passengers were dead, but there was a lot of blood and muddled thought.

In lieu of a winch, which would not have been long enough if we'd had one, Jake, Iglook, and guests Joe Dearmin and Jesse Bell, who were athletic and didn't smoke, took turns rappeling, hoisting and heaving all that half-dead weight to the surface. They said it was like climbing the Eiffel Tower with a steam turbine on your back.

Then they used the last of their ebbing strength to make a tree-to-creek search for the missing cab driver. (He was located later in the Hindquarter bar where, despite a badly dislocated shoulder, he'd crawled for help, been struck by amnesia and was downing boilermakers in an effort to remember his name and where on earth he'd come from.)

As smooth as Tinker to Evers to Chance, our guests stanched the most prominent wounds, formed stretcher parties and swiftly passed patients from hand to hand down to our living room. There Nurse Hurst slapped on bandages, pressure packs, splints, and slings like an eight-armed paperhanger.

Today Aspen has a multimillion dollar hospital with the finest emergency room and EMT crews in the business. Back then rescue work was strictly the homegrown, neighborhood, nonprofessional variety. With guests milling about dabbing slapdashedly at open wounds with our towels and jabbering about highway fatalities they had known, and Ken and Claytie leaning faintly in corners looking bilious, it was no wonder the poor survivors thought they'd fallen into a nest of international spies.

They were disoriented anyway, and it didn't help having Claytie giddily circle the room piping, "Would anyone care for a Tequila Sunrise? A Peppermint Twist?"

"Is she talking about a drink? Or does she want to dance?" asked one of the victims uncertainly.

"Dirty" Herwick, our sheriff and "the fattest gun in the West," arrived and did not help to restore order either. He was a kindly, well-intentioned man who would not have hurt a kitten, but his efforts were like shrapnel—best where they didn't hit. He kept trying to usher guest Jean Sandwick, who'd gotten mud and gore on her ski pants, into the sheriff's car under the mistaken impression that she was a walking wounded.

Finally Ellie howled like a banshee for everyone, except me and a few of our more collected women guests, to vacate the premises. "Out with the lot of you," she thundered. Under her efficient ministrations, method emerged from the maelstrom.

Most of the patients returned with casted arms and legs to thank us profusely. And several became eventual guests, insisting that our efficacious rescue work more than made up for our hideous road conditions.

As for the Heatherbed Lodge, we emerged infinitely the worse for wear. The next morning I surveyed a mountain of dirty linen imposing enough for an Iwo Jima flag raising. We never, *ever*, again sent out a klaxon call for sheets and towels.

Later we would haul an entire German ski club, five or six local high schoolers, an overeager trout fisherman, and Homer-Jaycox-on-a-toot out of that creek bed. What's more, all of the sirens luring the unwary onto our rocks were not down by the river.

One bright spring day Danny ran indoors calling, "Mom, there's a car. Upside down. In our drive."

"Are you sure you don't mean a turtle, Danny?"

"No, mom, a car. With people."

When I scurried outside, sure enough. A car lay on its

back like a beached paddle-wheeler, its tires spinning lazily in the air.

Motorists, transfixed by the sudden, enchanting glimpse of our colorful lodge in the trees below, were apt to veer over for a closer look and flip right off the edge. Eventually I grew very short-tempered about this, for despite a battery of Soft Shoulder and Dangerous Curve signs I browbeat Dirty into installing, drivers remained inexplicably incautious. I not only grew fed up with hauling out bandages, iodine, and my self-control, but also with guarding children, horses, and dogs in the eternal fear that someone might be squashed flat.

When our guests started risking their necks to leap from our precipitate premises of their own free will, I had no sympathy at all.

For reasons unclear to me, our architect designed the rear of the guest lounge, creekside, with massive sliding doors that led onto—nothing. Almost immediately our children discovered this quantum leap and began hurling themselves into the deep drifts below. Guests in their cups followed in their wake.

"Someone will KILL himself!" I cried to Ken.

"Nonsense, Martie. It's a straight drop into six feet of snow on a perfect level. Safer than a trampoline."

Nevertheless, I persuaded Ken to wire the doors shut.

But everytime he did, a besotted guest, contrived to unwire them and jump again.

Our friend Frank Bering owned and operated the Cloud Nine restaurant at the top of the Highlands. Frank cooked, ate and slept on Cloud Nine, and we attended many of his gala moonlight parties, skiing home through bright, moon-rippled snow. As far as I know, no one ever fell off the mountain. But one full moon night when we were having a gala of our own, Frank skied down and fell out of our lodge.

"Where's this famous lover's leap I've been hearing about?" he asked.

"It's not for lovers, it's for suicides, Frank. And it's wired shut. Have a drink and some of Ellie's famous Boston baked beans," I said.

Much later Frank, who'd skipped the beans and substituted a number of drinks, begged, "Aw, please, Martie, can't I try that jump?"

"Listen, Frank. This is March. The birds are nesting. The sun has melted the snow back there. It's mostly bare ground. Now be a good boy and let me fix you a ham sandwich." I patted him soothingly on the shoulder. "Maybe next year, after a nice heavy snowfall."

Much *much* later I heard "Ger-OOOOOOOOoooonn-i-mo!" and felt a familiar breeze at my back. "Oh my Lord," I whispered, afraid to look.

The next afternoon Frank skied down from Cloud Nine, dropped by the lodge, and peered at us through one black eye. "Say, what did I do last night? I'm as stiff as a poker and just as black."

When Ken showed Frank the plunge he'd taken, Frank's black-and-blue marks turned the color of ashes.

Another high-country hazard is the snowplow. Plows in those days were treacherous and operating one was as tricky as clutching a laying hen. A plow could snag and flip a three-quarter ton truck like a flapjack, and a driver had to know his terrain and his machine to avoid being catapulted into space. Ken was good at it, although he abused the art by detouring past Walt Smith's or Otto Steiner's or Teddy Armstrong's houses and plowing their cars under so they couldn't move for days. I accused him of feeling the same way about his plow as certain sophomoric males do about their toy trains. He not only kept our serpentine driveway plowed in heavy snows, he also rescued every stranded flatlander up and down our county road.

"Darn it, Ken, you've spent the last six nights hauling people out of ditches. And not one of them has given you the time of day, let alone a box of chocolates. You've got to tell them to call the tow services. Your children are growing up behind your back," I hammered at him.

Finally Ken got a crawful the week our "famous lawyer" came to ski.

When the Famous Lawyer arrived he introduced himself to one and all in exactly that fashion. On the telephone, "Hello, this is Theodore J. Trumpet, the famous lawyer from Paducah, Florida." To me, when we collided in the office as I was scurrying to check on a disconcerting odor of burning rubber issuing from the laundry room, "*I* am Theodore J. Trumpet, the famous lawyer from Paducah, Florida."

Lawyer Trumpet was indeed one of this country's most flamboyant trial lawyers, well-known for his brilliant defenses of the rich and the misbegotten. There was no need for him to toot his own horn. But he did, loudly, incessantly, and with the "1812 Overture" thundering in the background—to counterpoint piccolo twittering from the Playboy bunny draped over his Maximilian-furred arm. The bunny had the frozen expression of something out of Madame Tussaud's Waxworks, no doubt to preserve her makeup job *in vitro*. Nevertheless, she managed to emit astonishing roulades of gurgles, burbles, and tee-hees.

Theodore J. Trumpet was the large, unsilent type, a megalomaniac who expected the rise of courtroom excitement to greet his every entrance and red carpets to spring from planes and limousines to accept the tread of his mighty feet.

At first most of our guests breathed his name with awe. But after endless recitatives of trial, after trial, they grew increasingly fidgety. An evening with Ted was about as stimulating as a lecture on basket weavers of the Upper Volta.

I'd like to report that Ken and I were lawyer Trumpet's undoing. In fact it was Ma Bell that finally defeated him. Here was a man to whom a telephone was a physical extension of the right arm, and when he'd had enough of my expostulating, "I beg your pardon!" every time he slipped the phone deftly from my hand just as I was dialing our office supplier or the airport or a doctor, he called it quits. I'd long tried convincing him he'd be much better served in a nice Jerome Hotel suite with room service and phones, and at last he agreed. But not before his tootsie had turned half the cars in the place to wreckage.

Ted and Tootsie had been occupying the large room on the northwest corner of the lodge. Its big windows encompassed a view of creek and spruce trees, with a sidelong glance at the driveway dropping down to the lodge.

Tootsie was assiduous about her exercising. Apparently feeling that skiing and Ted Trumpet were inadequate as calisthenics (we couldn't imagine old Ted cavorting in bed with anything more stirring than the *Book of Torts*), she exercised regularly twice a day—at 8:30 A.M. and 4:30 P.M. on the button—in the buff, with the drapes undrawn, in full view of anyone starting down our steep incline. Word spread, and soon cars were lined in stately procession ready to crawl down that drive at 4:30 sharp.

The procession was not funereal enough for the men to double-check their verges. They kept nosing off the embankment like distraught B-52s. They then had to be dragged out and towed by their increasingly irritated lodge host. "If that floozy doesn't close her curtains or drape her frame, I'm going to dress her with my bare hands!" he stormed at me, as inflamed as a boil on a backside.

At length Trumpet and Strumpet packed up and moved. And despite my widely known phone phobia, I was delighted to restore communications with the outside world. As for Ken, he was finally cured of towing as a recreational pastime. Thereafter he limited himself to life or death efforts only.

*   *   *

As we have seen, the edges of Colorado country girdled far more than our modest lodge and its sheer surrounds. The atmosphere for miles featured unrailed mountain road, many antimacassar-sized summits of perpendicular mountains, and countless vertiginous hiking trails.

But my personal *bête noire* was the chairlift.

Mont Tremblant had the right idea. In order to spare early skiers' sensibilities, the Tremblant people built a wooden platform under the entire length of their main lift. They did not believe in yawning cavities that might give their pampered pioneers the idea they were gazing into the jaws of hell.

Here in Colorado our chairs not only cross dizzying hundred-foot drops, they are also possessed of maniacal animal instincts. They know when they are occupied by acrophobics and devout cowards. At just such moments they pause to sway sickeningly over awful gateways to perdition. And they lurch and dangle from a cable that, to one with chicken sensibilities, resembles a very loose thread.

While science prepares to clone Marilyn Monroe and robotize housework, couldn't someone out there devote a day or two to the chairlift? The damned things are still no stairway to the stars. Jumping on, into, or astraddle a moving lift can be as ticklish as jumping on a rolling log. I frankly would rather have an uneventful ride to the top of a ski mountain than do my spring sale shopping by computer chip. I just hate being irascible about this, especially with the chair the backbone of our livelihood. But darn it, every now and then somebody up there gets maimed, killed or frozen fast.

In the year of Our Lord 1960 I was one of them, and I still bear the emotional and other scars to prove it.

I had barely recovered from Brinkmanship rounds one through four when a ski day appeared disguised as heaven on earth. For a change I determined not to have a perfectly beautiful afternoon ruined by some great big back-breaking task, and I threw on my ski gear and rushed across the road.

The chair that then left the Highlands at Midway was approached by a steep wooden incline up which we all moved with our backs to the lift. Climbing briskly that sunstruck afternoon, I glanced ahead to count noses and saw that I would be paired with an attractive matron in a pink parka. (Color is an indispensable aid on the ski slopes—the fastest, surest way to pick out friends, ski patrol, your instructor, and bloodshed in vast expanses of white.)

I kick-stepped onto the lift platform just in time to leap into the chair and assume my position beside the lady in pink. What I had not seen was the patrolman who jumped the line from the other side, upset the count and put me into the double chairlift with the lady in pink and a gentleman in a blue funk. The lift operator, at the time, was picking his nose and gazing moodily at the skyline.

I am here (by the skin of my teeth) to tell you that those chairs will hold three people very cozily. My dingbat husband and his instructor cronies rode them *a trois* all the time, usually sandwiching in a giggling female powerless to defend herself. However, I had the misfortune to have joined a man who was a classic hysteric.

He did what I suppose he thought sensible at the time. He pushed me out.

When the lift operator ceased wondering for whom the bell tolled, realized it tolled for me, pulled the switch and stopped the lift, I was dangling by one arm over an eighteen-foot defile.

The only immediate sounds were the Pink Lady yelling at our chairmate, "You dumb son of a bitch, what'd you go and do that for?" and the whimpering of the dumb s.o.b. himself as he plucked limply at his armrest. The Pink Lady tried valiantly to haul me up into the chair. But she was hampered by my nerveless hands, me, and my thirty-four pounds of clothing and equipment. Unless you happen to be riding with Merlin Olsen, it is nearly impossible to pull yourself or anyone else back up into a chairlift.

It was also impossible to throw the machinery into reverse and reel me to safety.

A whole big bunch of spectators began swarming below and shouting a whole big bunch of worthless advice. With a sinking heart, I knew I'd have to drop. Eighteen feet may not sound like much to you armchair readers, but think of it as the roof of your house, and you'll have some idea of my dismay.

Thanking the Pink Lady for her concern, I rehearsed my moves. I made a mental note to flex my knees and roll fast; placed my skis tightly parallel; and, armed with prayer and clasping my hands like Al Jolson singing "Mammy," finally let go.

I discovered that hitting hardpack snow from that height is like running full tilt into a brick wall. I remembered to flex my knees, but I was far too jarred to roll. They slammed into my nose, peeling the skin like a taxidermist and splintering it to the consistency of bone meal.

Finding both legs sound, I refused aid from patrolmen or friends and stormed down that mountain madder than a wet hen. My pride hurt as much as my head, and if I'd encountered my chivalrous chairmate I would happily have snatched him bald. A slight dizzy spell at the bottom convinced me of the unwisdom of this, and I slunk home in the feeble hope that God would get him instead.

"Say, Mom, we heard that you . . ." cried the children excitedly as they rushed into the lodge from ski team practice. Slowly I lifted my ice pack and unveiled my face. Both eyes were swelling shut, my nose was spreading from ear to ear, and I was the color of spring violets and chocolate mousse. The children clammed up in perfect harmony and rushed about proffering cool cloths, hot drinks, and limpid, loving gazes.

Today, the ski world still has not united behind bigger and better chairlifts. And I'd really be grateful if you steel-trap minds would give this matter your immediate attention.

CHAPTER 17

Enroll Me
In Plumbing II-B

MARCH IS A month that veers from heavy spring blizzards
to warm luscious days that lap at your heels like tropic
surf and lure you to femoral fractures in the crusty spring
snow. In March we feel like characters from *Snowbound*
one minute and await geraniums and spring shine the
next. By March the wear and tear of winter begins taking
its toll of men and machines. Breakdowns among both
reach epidemic proportions.

We were to be faced with not one disaster, but with
dozens. They may have begun as a trickle, but they ended
in a tidal wave that would have swept Dorothy Lamour
off that Pacific island straight into the jaws of lost Atlan-
tis.

Just as the roses were reblooming amid Ellie's freckles
and she was close to mastering reverse shoulder turns, she
came in from the ski hill one afternoon and said, "Faith,
there's a tuuurrrible smell outside."

The tuuurrrible smell proved to be attar of septic tank,
and we rushed to the (fortunately empty) bunkrooms to
find the floors awash in a sea of bilge. Ken arrived from
ski school, took one sniff and uttered profanities I
wouldn't commit to this paper.

College spring vacations weren't due for ten days, and we didn't have anyone coming right in for those rooms. But that was *all* we had in our favor. Of course Ellie's hospital training came in handy once again, since she had a strong stomach and did not faint easily. As for me, like any woman with a number of children, I could stand the sight and smell of anything.

"I feel like Jean Valjean trapped in the sewer," I wheezed, emptying a bucket of sludge.

"Sure it's the work of the divvil," gasped Ellie, swabbing furiously with mops and rags.

"Listen, Ellie, if you're right, this place is probably haunted. What do you say we get in the car and leave for Las Vegas? Maybe no one will miss us."

"Hah!" she snorted.

We were caught in a clogged toilet without a plunger, and we knew it.

While Ellie and I labored mightily with mops and pails within, Ken called the Glenwood Septic Tank Company, and they advised as a first step that we locate the septic tank without. So Jake, Ken, and Jim Pomeroy began shoveling through deep drifts to reach rock-hard ground which they then painstakingly chiseled out by hand. Ellie and I may have toiled like Erie Canal men at a breach, but the poor men were tackling an undertaking comparable to defrosting an Artic ice cutter. Through that interminable night they cultivated an area the size of a battleship, searched for the malodorous tank and prayed that the Glenwood Septic Tank Company would appear as promised.

He did, at eight o'clock in the morning just as the men uncovered the guilty party. Together we thanked heaven for a downstream wind and no flies, and that the Glenwood Septic Tank Company did not turn tail and desert us.

It had required sixteen hours to uncover the low-down valve announcing in bold, orange letters: INLET. IN-

STALL ON TOP. (It was on the bottom.) Some six feet distant (naturally on top) was the valve lettered: OUTLET. INSTALL ON BOTTOM. The tank had been painstakingly disinterred upside down.

"It's in awful good shape," our plumber had described the slightly used tank to Ken. "Look at them stencils. Fresh as new." I don't know how he could tell. He had apparently obtained his license to practice despite total illiteracy.

Oh, well, the Glenwood Septic Tank Co. came equipped with an iron constitution, a two-ton truck with tank, and powerful pumps for just such emergencies as ours. With astonishing good will he trucked away tons of offal to I didn't dare ask where.

Visualizing the spread of giardia, botulism, Black Plague and white spider, Ellie and I fumigated, steam-sterilized and hand-scrubbed the inundated bunkrooms until our knucklebones gleamed through. Even the children rolled up their sleeves and helped, to the accompaniment of many "yeeeeecccccchs" and groans. Then we all staggered off to the showers.

Lodge crack-ups seemed always to catch us with an array of guests that would have made Barbara Howar ill with envy. Every skier in the house was invariably witty, stylish, and nondexterous with nary a man or woman (including the host and hostess) who knew a pipe wrench from a plumb bob. We had had a sewer contractor on the place only the week before the septic tank upheaval, and if we'd suspected what was in store, would have given him a lifetime's supply of lodging just to hang around awhile. (Later, as our popularity inexplicably increased in direct proportion to our breakdowns, we considered sending out mechanical aptitude tests with our reservation forms.)

When the days of infamy arrived, we had not so much as laid in a supply of spare parts, bottled water, votive candles, or blankets. (At the time we were both still young.)

Bill Beyer had warned Ken, "You'd better learn to be your own Mr. Fix-it, my friend."

"Lord, Bill, I hardly know a T-square from a thug bolt."

Bill sighed. "I suppose I can try showing you a few basics."

"Hell, I can always count on Fred Fisher," Ken said optimistically.

Freddie himself advised Ken as they foraged together at the dump one evening, "Aspen is no damn place for useless white-collar types, boy. You get yourself some coveralls and start working your way around the guts of that lodge, and you do it soon, before you have to perform major surgery."

At this early stage Ken and I were still devastated by the multifarious talent surrounding us. Every person in town seemed to have three college degrees, a native kinship with table saws, and a working knowledge of sod house construction, elemental physics, electric circuitry, bricklaying, and auto repair. Aspen seethed with indefatigable members of Mensa who staved off starvation with little things on the side: painting winter landscapes, baking Viennese pastries, welding steel sculpture, teaching Montessori, designing sportswear, mushing dogsleds, appearing in movies, and writing for magazines. It's no wonder we felt as inadequate as Presbyterian choir singers on the stage at La Scala.

I was no help to my husband. My flair for the mechanical was on a par with my affinity for advanced mathematics. Women who repaired their own stopped-up plumbing with a hairpin made me envious. To this day I use a can opener at the risk of severing an artery, and plugging in a table lamp depletes me.

Ken had taken a few faltering steps toward becoming a more accomplished Aspenite. Using a mail-order instruction manual, he had wired some outside lights without sending us up in geysers of blue flame. He was so pleased with himself you would have thought he'd mined the copper, hand-knit the filaments, and been sanctified by the American Society of Electrical Workers.

Our initial aggravations with the lodge were minor but just that—aggravating. One indicator of greater perfidies to come was our handsome brass door locks. Claytie, who was accustomed to arriving home at the thermometer's nadir between three and five A.M., announced that she was fed up with fumbling tearfully over a useless room key at ten degrees below zero. "Father, those keys simply will not turn, my hands turn into mummy claws, and if I peel off any more skin I'll be playing boogie and bop with my bare bones."

If Claytie had been alone in her complaints, we'd have laid the blame squarely where it belonged—on a Democratic congress and too many double Scotches. But other guests were also freezing fast in the act of unlocking room doors. After we'd summoned Freddie from a warm bed or hot saxophone several dozen times, he finally said, "Let's replace the son-of-a-bitching things. I may pick locks, but that doesn't mean I like taking candy from babies."

As time went by we began to suspect that our lodge and all its components were lemons. But unlike a car, you can't very well trade a ski lodge in on a new model.

In case of emergency, we found, one did not thumb through the yellow pages and willy-nilly pick out an electrician, plumber, roof man, pipe, or heating man. For one thing, the yellow pages were no thicker than my thumbnail. For another, there was seldom more than one of anything, and he was always busy. As Bill Beyer and Fred Fisher had forewarned, Ken faced the sobering fact that he was trapped in a mare's nest of wiring and plumbing, and it was up to him to fight his way out alone.

The biggest crosses we bore involved the loss of heat and hot water. Over the next few years, as Heatherbed veterans stood about on gelid feet tossing off drinks and brave one-liners while waiting for showers to steam or rooms to warm, Ken and I dispensed more booze on the house than Texas Guinan in her prime.

In point of fact, we started out with limitless quantities of hot water. It was just that hundreds of gallons of the stuff were being filtered into toilets or siphoned through the cold water faucets.

We first became aware of this unhappy diversion when Bob Pullen, our favorite Houstonian, complained that he'd have to check into Menninger's for his hangovers if we couldn't accommodate them. "I knew I shouldn't have ordered those stingers after dinner," he moaned. "But it isn't right for a man to clutch his sink and sob while he waits twenty minutes for scalding steam to expend itself so he can have a life-giving Alka Seltzer in a glass of reasonably cool water."

Ken feverishly dismantled walls, cursed, called Freddie, cursed, pounded joists, cursed and at last bellowed, "Found the bastards." He had no sooner located the bungled hot and cold connections than he uncovered a problem to make a pontiff weep. Our hot and cold water pipes had been laid cozily side by side, with only light insulation (which soon deteriorated) between. They had then been entombed in the four-foot cement foundation of the building. "I'm surprised the plumbers didn't lay a 'Rest In Peace' wreath down there," Ken announced bitterly. No wonder much of our water was an unsatisfactory amalgam, too warm for drinking, too cool for bathing.

As far as we know, there is no hope of exhuming those pipes to this day, short of burning the lodge to the ground and pulverizing the foundation with nitroglycerin. We solved the problem less dramatically, though at great expense, by adding an entirely new network of pipes. Above ground.

Within a few weeks of the septic tank, frozen locks, and tepid water debacles, I hurriedly wrenched on the kitchen faucet and was rewarded with a sickening trickle. Sickening trickles had appeared before, and they've appeared since. But I for one need my disasters spread thin. When they cluster like migraines I lose touch with reality. My vision blurs at the edges. I see quick-darting gophers that are not there.

"I can't face people one more time," I cried and collapsed in a piteous heap on our bed.

If I have not mentioned this before, I will state here and now that skiers as a species are the most generous, sportsman-like, considerate, uncomplaining group of kindred souls on the face of the earth. When nuclear cataclysm strikes, skiers should be saved to repopulate the earth. Fighting elements and lift lines brings out their heroic traits. And if, in addition, they stayed at our lodge, they developed backbones like elevator shafts.

The week of the trickle every man, woman, and child refused to desert us. Except for Claytie, who with the sure instincts of a rat on a sinking ship, fled for Ulla Nillson's warm beds, hot water, and heat. "I will be right back when you and Father have things repaired." she promised. "Right now my nerves are frayed, and of course you don't want me dragging around with a long face."

Bob Quistgard, lovable Minnesota druggist, insisted brightly that brushing his teeth with vodka really got him going for the day. Louise Tyrer, M.D., announced that bathing only opens the pores to disease and too much washing is a twentieth-century menace. Doctors Ray Anderson and Ray Van Cleve issued water tumblers of straight whiskey with an Rx for Sterlings and staff to "drink every drop p.e.r."

In the interim, our physician guests lectured us sternly on stress and hardening of the arteries. (At this point my arteries were the consistency of burled oak.) We Sterlings looked so haggard that our skiers, bless them, worried about *us*. They bolstered our morale with stories of no water in Cuernavaca, no water at the Caribe Hilton, and no water in French Lick. This helped, but not much. There's an awful immediacy about no water *here* right *now*.

In truth, our water, all stemming from those natural springs on the side of the abrupt descent into our Lower Forty, was always reliable and always there. I didn't understand it then, and I still don't today. Out of those springs and into a one-thousand-gallon holding tank poured fresh mountain water positively bursting with vitamins and minerals (minerals which, in a very short time, corroded all our pipes, thus leading to another chapter of sickening trickles). From the holding tank the water flowed through pipes, which, thanks be to God, never froze, and thence into a pressure tank on the slope below the lodge, where a pump pumped it up to the buildings and our guests' waiting fingertips. It was on the last lap of the journey that that water ran into our pitiful in-house plumbing.

Since it was impossible for Ken to enroll in night school, he learned on the job. While our lodgers chopped roof ice to wet their parched lips, bathed like Spartans or not at all and wrapped chilled blue bodies in borrowed quilts, he spent a thousand and one nights under a foot of freezing water searching for a lost tank plug; bleeding air that gathered because the foot valve in the pressure tank disintegrated; dismantling the furnace pump; stilling the demented leaps of boggled pipes; and soldering leaks in the water mains. Through it all he managed to keep joking on the outside. Inwardly he felt as if he'd been force-fed two pounds of chocolate-covered cherries.

For a while water became such an obsession that I considered canning it in fifty-gallon drums.

Closely related to the water problems was the heat. Coal stokers, we were glibly informed when we built, were nowadays efficient, trouble free, clean, economical, and "Absolute Jewels." That's what the heating man (a blood brother to the septic tank man) solemnly swore, looking me deep in the eyes. "Them stokers is Absolute Jools, Miz Sterling. You and the mister won't believe the job this beauty will do."

Because natural gas had not yet been piped our way, we really didn't have a choice. We installed one.

For roughly six months the Absolute Jool was efficient, trouble free, clean, and economical. Then, token duty done, it clogged up, coughed, smoked, bogged down, emitted clouds of coal gas and settled into permanent semi-invalidism. Like it or not, Ken became intimately acquainted with the innermost workings of that big black bastard. On bitter cold nights his ministrations were often necessary at three-hour intervals, and we were back on the same schedule as when the children were babies.

Bob Pullen and Ross Grimes and their long-suffering wives were in residence the night our heat first failed us. The men appeared swathed in blankets to hail us out of bed with the news that they were at Ice Station Zero. Although the rest of the lodge was toasty, their particular rooms were the temperature of polar ice packs.

"I'd hate to think you were deliberately driving us out," Ross said. "Tell me, is it my underarm odor?" shivered Bob.

"This is no time for jokes, you clods," growled Ken, jumping into his pants. He summoned Freddie and, with many heart-warming oaths, they found that the hot water baseboard heaters were developing air locks which very neatly shut off a room's heat supply. Thereafter when shivering guests knocked on our door at four in the morning, Ken leapt wordlessly to his feet, strapped on his squeaking leather tool belt and manfully rushed to the valves. He became so practiced that he could bleed out a baseboard and restore our guests' heat and equanimity without fully regaining consciousness.

Because there were no sealed heat systems at that time, it wasn't long before not only individual rooms, but the lodge in its entirety began to go.

The first time this happened Claytie was entertaining. She had enticed Teddy Wilson, the great jazz pianist, into finishing his gig in town and moving out to the Heatherbed for a two A.M. encore. The encore stretched into the next morning and right through the following afternoon. After all, there was no reason for Teddy to move a thing but his fingers. He was plied with food, drink, and adulation by a worshipful Claytie. And then too the man was undoubtedly frozen fast to the piano bench.

When Claytie burst into our bedroom shortly before dawn (she never knocked), bundled in furs and as touchy as a panda in heat, she exclaimed, "Really, Father, I do think you're carrying this economy kick too far. My fingers are like talons, and that dear, delectable Teddy Wilson says he's going to open a few blood vessels to provide some heat."

"Wh-whaaaaaaazat?" Ken said, struggling up through frosty air.

"Even with the fireplace roaring, our bones are clanking like ice cubes."

"Oh, God," prayed Ken, leaping convulsively from the bed.

Well, one icy room at a time may have been hell on the occupants, but at least it could be remedied without discommoding large bodies of people. The lodge frozen in its entirety was a calamity more on a Mount Rushmore scale. Reheating a sizable Aspen edifice in midwinter is like trying to defrost the state of Maine. On that initial occasion Teddy Wilson, like the men who went down with the Titanic, played on. While Ken struggled at the barricades, Ellie and I bore our nonmusical guests off to the Jerome for a very long, very expensive champagne breakfast.

"That Claytie is dotty as a dodo, but thank heaven for her late hours," Ken sighed exhaustedly when heat was fully restored. "Things would have been a lot worse if we'd waited much longer."

There is nothing more trying for a bone-tired, out-of-shape vacationer than dragging back to one's lodging only to face the spectre of no hot water, *no hot water whatsoever*. Under those conditions, he may never calm himself enough to sleep again.

Builders, architects, plumbers, and amateur observers by the score had assured us in lyric tones that a five-hundred-gallon hot water heater with the new "jet recovery" would be more than adequate for our needs. Well, they were wrong and it wasn't. Not when thirty-five chilled skiers arrived home from the hills in tandem and dove for the showers in two-four time. At length we sheepishly asked everyone please to stagger their bathing. The water heater and the Absolute Jool were simply not quick enough about recovering their wits. Unless a guest darted in and out like a dragonfly, his final rinse was apt to be a plunge à la Polar Bear Club.

Dick McKaughan naturally seized every opportunity to inquire of those assembled, "Has anyone here heard what we pay for a room with hot water?"

When natural gas found its way to us, we were among the first weepingly grateful customers. The Big Black Jool, with accompanying grates, firebox, belts, and gears joined a large company of other abandoned stokers at the town dump. When I made tentative inquiries about a trade-in, the same furnace man who had looked me in the eye and sworn, "Them stokers is Absolute Jools, Miz Sterling," now stated severely around his chaw, "Them stokers is like assholes, ma'am. Ever-body has one, don't a soul need two." "I'll just bet that guy got his training in used cars," I swore heatedly to Ken. And thus another of our initial solid investments passed into ignominious oblivion.

And you know, we didn't care. We were so happy reveling in a plethora of heat, hot water, and uninterrupted sleep that we didn't care if we were dragged off to bankruptcy court, giggling and cavorting like loons.

CHAPTER 18

Ski Bums We Have Loved

RIGHT AFTER Easter, Jim and Jake kissed us good-bye and took off for a month of surfing in Mexico. Ellie's work ethic sent her to the Aspen Hospital until the next season of elk stew and deficits would recall her to the Heatherbed. With our last guests gone, we were suddenly reduced to a paltry family of eight. It was my first taste of the empty nest syndrome—only in this case the fledglings were still around and it was the strong right arms of our ski bums that I missed.

The ski world may not know it, but it is infinitely poorer without the Mom-and-Pop lodge that once upon a time operated on love and ski bum power. Such hostelries have become as quaint as watermills. Rising in their stead are the condominiums of today, where the skier is bereft forever of that old-fashioned ambience where guests gathered to swap lies, to find happiness with total strangers, and to know the ski bum.

During our race to finish building the Heatherbed, friends had explained the procedure for hiring help: interview every clean-cut, strong-backed, eager young thing who turned up around Thanksgiving and pick out the likeliest prospects. Over the years our successful applicants ran the gamut of social strata from Park Avenue playboy to ex-con, and we found only two types not gen-

189

erally viable: Southern belles and anyone under sixteen. The belles were darlings and good workers, but invariably fell in love with bachelor guests and departed starry-eyed to look at engagement rings in the city. Kids under sixteen suffered from lack of direction and underdeveloped senses of humor.

Ken and I were equal opportunity employers. All sexes and creeds not daunted by the sight of small children and unmade beds were warmly welcome. Naturally we turned down anyone with bony, dope-weakened shoulders or mossy teeth, and we abjured Latin dancer types who looked as if they'd ooze in and out of guest rooms after cleaning hours. In general we preferred nondomestic types from nice wholesome families—kids who could carry a tune, a conversation, loads of laundry, and firewood with uniform aplomb. But we hired just about the first hale and hearty applicants who didn't say "youse guys" and who passed muster with the children.

The children may have been too puny for heavy lodge work, but survival in a large family had made them superior judges of character. Dan and DearGwen, when six and nine respectively, warned me that a Dutch girl I'd hired would never have the stomach for the job.

"She's scared of bugs, mom," Gwendy said scathingly.

"She's gonna pay me to catch the ground spiders in her bathtub," Dan announced disbelievingly. (Ground spiders breed in high-altitude water pipes, and fresh litters climb up the drains with alarming regularity.) Of course the children themselves contributed plenty to Heintje's undoing.

Nevertheless they were right. She was so terrified of spiders, flies, snakes, mice—anything she felt had fangs and might leap out and attack without provocation—that she was soon a jittering wraith.

Ski lodges in those days were not only rough-hewn, they were not hermetically sealed. With the onset of winter, anything that could crawl in out of the snow, did. In lieu of clearing Heintje's tub of spiders and her closet of nesting field mice, the children filled quart Mason jars with hibernating bugs and trapped every sluggardly snake for miles, releasing them in the hapless Heintje's quarters. Certain she'd come to rest in a zoological holding tank, the girl fled home to Holland.

Heintje was the exception. Far more usual was the young Trojan willing to endure any privation to ski. Unlike his suave predecessor, the tennis bum (known for sharing the soft beds of country club daughters and bankers' wives), the ski bum was content to live in a slab-sided cabin, sleep on a hard bunk and feed himself, preemployment, on restaurant leftovers.

Our own bums were never put to such rigorous tests. They immediately became members of the family and shared our low-income, high-protein diet of wildlife (the children always claimed that we smelled like the San Diego zoo when we burped) and Lilliputian living quarters, with fifteen inches of closet space per person. At the Heatherbed we practiced togetherness with the tact of submariners.

Our novitiates got the education of their young lives. They learned to expect five or ten extra for dinner, to stretch a salad until it squeaked, to make a pie, cake, or quiche serve fourteen instead of eight. They mastered the fundamentals of castle keeping, learned to put together parties for two hundred on an afternoon's notice and tackled the mysteries of child rearing with frequently ragged results. Our bums further learned to brew coffee for eighty instead of eight; to build large, efficient fires and, not infrequently, put them out; wash, dry and fold enough linen to fill all the sarcophagi of Egypt; unthaw frozen pipes; introduce single guests to likely dates; isolate troublemakers and neutralize bores; resolve marital tiffs; and keep smiling though dog-tired, sick of small talk, and wondering what in God's name possessed them to leave Schenectady.

After that they had to endure Wednesday nights.

Wednesday nights were a minor social hell for which the children were scrubbed until they looked waxed and buffed, dressed in their best, and made to practice mixing drinks, passing hors d'oeuvres, minding their manners, and speaking French at the dinner table. (Robin swears that when introduced to the French Ambassador in Tehran the year she was thirty she chirruped, "*Passez le beurre, s'il vous plaît.*") Fearing the West would rub all the polish off our little nuggets, I clung to this idiotic tradition for years.

In the beginning we were taken aback by the many young men who offhandedly applied for work as "domestics." Of course this was early Women's Lib and those were troubled times. It was not yet acceptable for well-brought-up youngsters to drop out of college for a semester, and girls less so than boys. Unless a girl was recovering from a broken engagement or a clandestine pregnancy, she was expected to carve out her B.A. without any damn fool pauses for refreshment.

Most of our first bums, like Jake, were recently discharged from the army. Or, like Ellie, already finished with school. Iglook leaned toward the army crowd. They could miter a sheet tight enough to bounce a quarter roof high, and KP duty had hardened them to the rigors of the kitchen. I always felt girls were better at spotting cobwebs festooning the rafters. But at those prices we didn't expect the perfect hybrid of Jeeves and Hazel.

Starting with Jake and Ellie, we got more than our money's worth. They not only chopped forests of cordwood and distributed mountains of sheets, but also carried on despite such occupational hazards as ski fractures, barked-on-bedframes shins, luggage lifter's hernia, and middle-of-the-week hangover. When I was afflicted with muddy thinking, they took over the whole megillah.

Ken's and my routine differed from our ski bums' in

just one respect: they skied in the afternoon, we seldom had a moment to ourselves. When Ken skied it was to instruct twittering matrons or querulous oldsters for Stein. When I skied it was after the reservation mail was answered; sick children, animals, and guests were doctored; the lodge or dinner or both were not on fire; our skier capacity was very low; I had an ounce of strength left in my wobbly legs; or favorite guests bullied me into it. I felt very fortunate to ski two or three times a month.

"How marvelous to have your own ski lodge and snow and mountains," guests would trill. To them our life appeared like a sojourn in Davos. In reality our seasons were like training for a heavyweight title bout, with guess who as the punching bag?

The lodge work was inexorable. Unless one of us was hugely incapacitated, we were loathe to saddle the others with their own and our share of the chores. All of us staggered through the days and nights like steeplechasers taking bumps, jumps, and water holes.

Ken and I, having passed into our thirties, didn't always have the stamina for the job. We counted on our bums to fill our shoes, more often than they suspected. In return, we treated them as prized members of the establishment and expected our guests to do the same. Urged on by our unsubtle room directives, the guests got the message. They befriended our bums, tipped them magnanimously and invited them home to Fort Worth the following summer.

A doctor or a nurse in a hotel is as hard to hide as a case of measles. That first year both Ellie and Uncle Whit, after tending to the family, seemed always to be dispensing medications and instructions to lineups of guests with chest colds, altitude sickness, aching fractures, sprains, strains, and leaky sinus tracts.

As for Jake, he was so adaptable that he kept right on working and skiing with not just one but two broken legs.

He was an active participant in a local game of Russian Roulette called "The Bash For Cash," in which racers started in a body from the top of a narrow Highlands course and streaked for the bottom trampling each other en route. He was rarely out of plaster for long. He simply cut down his walking casts, strapped on boots with long thongs, wore outsized jeans and continued schussing the mountain and hustling luggage as though totally fused. He became so practiced as a cripple that when attacked by a drunk in the Abbey Bar he knocked the guy cold with a karate chop of his leg cast.

In addition to a high I.Q. and great athletic prowess, Jake possessed a cabalistic appeal for animals, small children, and older women. Our kids adored him. He was a tough and loyal worker, a gentle giant who, in his off-hours, fought off enamored women who wanted his body and besotted men itching for a fight. After he went to work for the ski patrol, he was always available when we needed him to ride in a horse race, catch us a mess of trout, lodge-sit or put out fires.

Robert Vandeveer "Chip" Stone IV arrived with his mother our second Thanksgiving and, like the Man Who Came to Dinner, stayed until Easter. Chip was one of those highbred young men born with Guccis on their feet and blood that tested a deep navy blue. He was as different from Jake as a borzoi is from a bull terrier. At the wizened old age of twenty he'd been given the glove at both Choate and Yale, crewed yachts from Monaco to Martinique, taught ballroom dancing, acted in movies and was on intimate terms with the "Right People" in tonier watering holes around the world. He was devastatingly handsome, brimming with charm, and a little awe-inspiring for one so young. In fact his wealth of dazzling experience made me entertain serious doubts about my own pale, wasted life—although none of it struck me as useful preparation for being a chambermaid.

194

When he drawled that he thought it would be "good fun" ski bumming for a season, my innermost voice muttered, Oh, no you don't. I could see him lying in our beds, never making them.

"I'd really welcome the opportunity to polish my skiing," he purred.

"The only things we polish around here are brass, copper, and furniture," I snapped churlishly.

Before I could spirit Ken away for one of our little marital chats, he weakened and hired him. Apparently he detected attributes in Chip that escaped me completely. Since the boy easily passed muster with the children, I had no recourse but to sit back and simmer.

Chip proved to be one of our all-time Grade A ski bums.

That kid could have put a Baptist minister at ease in a seraglio. Before long we felt very fortunate having him organize our small, disoriented ski lodge instead. He mopped floors, made beds and washed windows with jaunty dispatch (and frequent assistance from unattached young females). He was also tireless in fulfilling our guests' every wish.

He escorted powder skiers straight to the only untracked terrain for miles, hosted picnics for which he selected the truffles and vintage wines, packed the napery and chose out-of-the-way mountain sites with incomparable vistas. He taught leaden-footed older women to samba divinely and, with one guest or another in tow, entered and won every twist contest in town; coaxed slew-footed men into vedelning like Norse pixies; and coached spoiled children in winning at gin and backgammon, instead of pestering their elders. Half-Whit became such a card shark under Chip's expert tutelage that we had to call a halt to gambling with guests. The child was fleecing them right and left.

Our youngsters were as enslaved as our skiers. Their conversations ran along the lines of, "Mother, Chip says if I'm going to enroll in a decent school like Miss Porter's

we'd better get cracking. He may have to pull strings."
(This from Robin.)

"Abercrombie's has some neat foils I'd like for my
birthday. Chip has the catalogue in his room." (Mike)

"Abercrombie who?"

"You know, Abercrombie & Fitch. Chip's teaching me
to fence."

"On whose time?" (Me, darkly.)

"Say, Mom, Chip says we should learn about RPMs
and down-shifting. Do you think we could practice on Dr.
Smedley's Porsche?"

"No, Whit, I do *not* think you could practice on Dr.
Smedley's Porsche, not even when you get your driver's
license in another six years!" I yelled, my voice changing
gears and shifting into high.

One evening Gwyneth and Deirdre asked me anxiously
what I planned to do about introducing them.

"To whom?" I inquired absentmindedly as I unraveled
another knot in my knitting.

"You know," said Gwendy, "our debuts."

At that point I was testier than a waitress in tight shoes,
and I stalked off to collect Chip for a good firm heart-to-
heart.

"Listen, friend," I told him, "the kind of thing you're
promoting is just what we brought the children west to
escape. Keep filling their little heads with uppercrust ap-
plesauce, and the next thing we know they'll be demanding braised unicorn for breakfast."

Chip allowed as how the Rockies were certainly not the
Hamptons and maybe I had a point.

Despite these adverse influences on the young, Chip
was nearly the complete and perfect ski bum. A superb
Aspen vacation is compounded of glorious skiing, fine
food and wines, exciting après-ski life, congenial new
friends and/or romances, and general refortification for
another year back at the factory. Chip was a genie who
made all these dreams come true. Our guests that winter

left town giddily replete, certain they'd completed a seminar in Shangri-la.

Over the years we've followed Chip's travels in the snootier periodicals and were not surprised to read he'd been skiing Zermatt with the Agha Khan. "And no doubt screwing up the poor guy's turns," sniffed Half-Whit, by that time an older, slightly jaded ski champion with his own Alfa Romeo and license to drive it.

"Joy Baby" Schaleben was the daughter of the editor of the *Milwaukee Journal*, and one of the four darling Wisconsin students who'd replaced the Witlesses our first Christmas. When Ken discovered them subsisting on peanut butter sandwiches so they could afford our cheap bunkroom rates and their lift tickets, he put them to work chopping kindling and serving gluehwein après-ski. In exchange he gave them free lodging and invited them to our apartment for a nourishing meal of elk stew with dumplings. From that day forward Joy Baby, her immediate family, her in-laws, and her legions of friends constituted a sizable labor pool of Heatherbed "regulars." One or another of them turned up between post-graduate work, boring jobs, moving from coast to coast, or backpacking around Yugoslavia to ski bum with us for another season.

One lazy autumn afternoon when we were in the horse business up to the withers, I had just finished helping Ken pack a large, jovial group going into the high country to leaf watch—and I was feeling morose at being left behind with all those unmade beds and unbridled children, when Joy Baby drove down the driveway on her way to California. "You godsend," I whooped and handed her the lodge keys. In fifteen minutes she had settled into the office as if it were a well-worn, comfortable shirt, and I was off on the pack trip. Our other guests never even suspected the place had changed hands. Those were the kind of ski bums we knew and loved.

The unlikeliest bums we ever had were Claytie and Ulla. It was late in the season, the children had unwittingly become the western distributors of chicken pox, and Ellie was among their first customers. That same week Jake injured another leg. Having everyone covered in plaster or a communal rash is about as good for the hotel business as a death in the house. I was slumped in the kitchen, wondering how on earth I'd make all those beds and mop so many fevered brows, when Claytie chirped, "Do not despair, dear one. Ulla and I will be *happy* to do the room work."

"Come on, Claytie," I bristled, "you can't even climb out of bed before the cocktail hour."

"Just point me at the brooms and brushes, Martha Jane, and we'll see about that!" she snapped.

Although Ken and I were prepared to go it alone, I was astonished to find Claytie rummaging through the linen closet at *nine o'clock the following morning.*

"I may faint," I gasped.

"Well, don't, we need all hands here," she barked. Her personality had undergone the same change as her hours.

Claytie, got up in a white apron, silk scarf, her ubiquitous cigarette holder, and an elaborate feather duster, bore a striking resemblance to Auntie Mame slumming at a firehouse supper. Nevertheless, thanks largely to Ulla's robust constitution, the two of them actually got the work done. For a few days.

Then, one morning as I was rebandaging a guest's ankle sprain, Claytie stalked into the lounge like Madame de Farge and demanded, "*Who* is in room nine?"

There was a startled silence. Finally Mavis Webster, a sweet, housewifely type, said meekly, "We are."

"Well, my dear, you get four gold stars. You have made your bed and tidied up and everything is in apple pie order. I owe you two double Scotches on the house." Whereupon Claytie turned and marched from the room while

I felt myself go hot, then cold, and fell to examining an old family water color as though I had never laid eyes on it in my life.

The next day all the guests in the lodge had acquiescently made their beds before leaving for the ski hill.

"Caroline Clayton Calhoun Ethridge," I later stormed, "you have coerced these nice people into working themselves to the bone on their own vacations."

"But of course. I had no idea that maidwork was so exhausting. This is an emergency."

"I don't give a damn if it's a five-alarm fire, those people came here for a rest and a change, and that's what they're going to get."

"Oh pooh, Martha Jane. I'm throwing a Bloody Mary and *huevos rancheros* party on Saturday, and all the guests are purely delighted."

Not nearly so delighted as I was to have Ellie and Jake back on their feet and the job.

At the end of our first ski season my toenails ached, I had pains in what the Infant called my "eyebrowns," and Ken and I were ready to be laid to rest in the old Ute cemetery.

Skiers may be a wondrous breed, but a skier on vacation expects every night to be New Year's Eve. Sharing in this total hilarity, we found, meant courting alcoholism and mental breakdown. This was not our guests' fault. We exuded so much hearty good will that they thought of us as human dynamos who only incidentally had a family to rear and a ski lodge to operate.

For our ski bums the high, clear air of the Rockies was, at first, like stepping out of an asbestos factory into an oxygen tent. For a while they had energy to waste. But even in their healthy young primes, the best of them were pretty burned out by spring. The most chubby-cheeked took on the interesting facial planes and gaunt expressions of Cherokee Indians. By the end of our first season there was a detectable pallor just beneath Jake's and Ellie's Moroccan leather tans.

Yet over the years we found that after long, dull summers of store clerking or ditch digging, Judy, Rick, Jim, Ben, Scotty, Ingrid, Cary, Cookie, and Steve—like Jake and Ellie—forgot the rigors and remembered the rewards. Many of them reappeared on our doorstep any old time of the year, usually with a friend in tow. Sometimes we felt as if we were the sole moral and financial support of vast numbers of itinerants who drifted in and out of our lives like empty bottles bobbing around an island. We hosted (and usually footed the bill for) the weddings of numbers of ski bums who told us, tears in their eyes, that we were the only real family they'd ever known. We acted as honorary godparents to countless newborns. We offered an ever-ready haven for the jilted, the divorced, and the bereaved.

One of our girls met her future husband in the deep end of our swimming pool; another, an associate producer who gave her a start in movies. An ex-nun opted, with visible relief, to return to the cloister. Among our graduates are an oral surgeon, a world-class race driver, a freelance writer, assorted business tycoons, dozens of workaholics, and only one known failure. We're especially pleased with our happily married couples. Lord knows they learned from us everything they'll ever need to know about burden sharing and borderline survival.

Many of our kids returned, finding it difficult to grow up, and away from, the special magic of Aspen. But for the average, well-adjusted ski bum, one season was plenty. By April they were accomplished, often spectacular skiers, polished housekeepers, and ready to make some nice boy or girl very happy.

One way or another, we like to think that we had a lasting effect on a whole lot of young lives.

CHAPTER 19

The Cruelest Month

SOMETIME IN April Aspen closes its lifts and officially kisses winter good-bye. The thing is, winter doesn't always go quietly. Often she loiters like the last guest at a party, loathe to depart. But although we can expect contrary spring snows into May and often June, the giant thaws have long begun.

Aspen in April is at her absolute worst, a disheveled housewife on her way to a garage sale. Her hair needs shampooing, her petticoats show, her stockings sag. I mean, she's a mess.

That first spring, Ken and I treaded marshlands of glutinous mud, feeling like Chloe in the swamp. The children scarcely noticed, except for their mother's distraught howls to halt and strip at the back door.

There was mud in the parking lots, driveways, and sidewalks. Mud crept into the post office, stores, schools, houses, pockets, bookshelves, silver drawers, and beds. When our minister's wife stopped by for a cup of coffee and an encouraging word, she had a grimy face, two grubby children, and the off-season blues. "I don't know, Martie," she said, "it all seems so futile." I scrubbed a blotch of dirt from her cheek, reminded her that summer was around the corner and sent her on her way wondering who was ministering to whom.

As the communal morass settled deeper, and unpalatable gray snowbanks slowly trickled into oblivion, any number of things came to light: those great, ugly piles of builder's debris left around the Heatherbed last December, empty beer cans, wine bottles, cigarette butts, Miss Strumpet's other earring, cocktail glasses, sun goggles, fly rods, flat tires, candy wrappers, thousands of matchbooks, kindling, lodging brochures, junior racing schedules, used razor blades, empty soft drink cartons, abandoned lunches, old lift tickets, watches, chain mail, and worn wimples.

Townspeople raked, hoed and bulldozed this cumulative trash in the direction of the county dump. And our posse joined the gangs of enterprising youngsters out scouring the ground beneath the lift towers. There they turned up an astounding assortment of petty cash and dropped valuables. One Sunday morning, Mike and Whit triumphantly bore home eight jeroboams of Dom Perignon champagne. "Look at this, you guys," they crowed, "a neat present, and we even uncorked it for you."

Frenziedly we called Ria, Bill, Mrs. Packard, Mariellen, Sheila, and any of our friends still in residence and cried, "Drop everything and come right over for champagne and Cheerios."

Whoever warbled inanely about "Springtime in the Rockies" must have had his mountains mixed up. Like molasses in January, spring creeps very slowly toward the Colorado high country. Bare, unsavory branches surreptitiously turn a pale, shimmering green to match the wild asparagus by the roadsides. Shy cinquefoil, gentian, and creekside alders send tentative buds into the raw, uncourteous air. Spotted sandpipers appear cautiously among the catkins, in creeks edged with ice and swollen with runoff. Elk and bighorns, after cadging handouts from ranchers through the winter, begin slowly working their way up to treeline.

At lower altitudes, the ranches are suddenly vast maternity wards overflowing with shivering newborns. We took the children down-valley to see ewes being sheared, to watch the lambing and to pick out "bummer" lambs for their 4-H projects. Newborn colts staggered about on wobbly legs, and baby calves frisked and tumbled behind their mothers. Despite Mother's stern admonitions we succumbed to the children's pleas and bought our first two horses: a nine-year-old quarterhorse named Chief, who was to carry legions of kids through barrel, pole, and roping events; and Carryall, an aloof thoroughbred jumper who obviously thought us beneath her station. We even considered breaking Nemnon, the half-tame elk who hung around pilfering our horses' hay, to the saddle so he could earn his keep.

On one of those sun-drenched days that cajoles you into thinking this is really July, we packed a picnic and climbed Red Butte, that anomalous razorback rising from the glacial moraine to the northwest of town. We perched precariously atop its saddle summit amid ancient crustaceans from an inland sea and surveyed still snow-locked mountains in our bathing suits.

We became acquainted for the first time with the neighborhood harbinger of spring. Nutty George was a hard-billed, crusty old woodpecker who showed up every April to get back to work on the creosoted telephone pole at the top of our driveway. The woods were loaded with towering pines and murmuring spruce, wormy and rotten to the core. But George kept whamming away at that stone-cold telephone pole in his same old psychotic style. We were crazy about the dumb bird.

During the giant hangover that precedes summer, every Aspenite with a dollar to his name and a brain in his head surveys the depredations of the ski season and opts for a respite in the tropics. The stay-in-Aspens who slog through the mire looking grubby and feeling low, grow fewer and fewer. Before tackling the housecleaning, people slam and lock the doors and head south to Mexico, Papeete, the Caymans, anywhere they can lean back and watch bougainvillea grow.

At the end of our first April Ken and I farmed out the children and managed a leisurely look at the Southwest. In Santa Fe we visited Indian pueblos and stayed at the Bishop's Lodge, where Jim Bishop treated us to a lovely respite "on the house." We strolled through the Petrified Forest, basked in Navaho sun and peered over the edges of the Grand Canyon, which for some reason made me homesick.

We were on hand, however, for the ride to the top of the Highlands for Easter sunrise services. It was a moving moment, seeing the world reborn from the peak of a Rocky Mountain. We skied down through Charley Horse snow—the kind that grabs your skis, jolts you into unexpected gears and has you praying that you won't break a leg. Not here, not now, not at the start of another, busier season.

Colorado's spring snow makes Hamlet's Denmark look as solid as Gibraltar. It is so rotten that stern measures are called for. By the end of March, avalanche blasting reaches the proportions of military exercises. Our dogs never learned to accept this calmly. With the first explosion, they would streak into the house to hide quivering like whippets under the beds and office desk.

Colorado's San Juan Range alone has some three thousand recorded avalanches per winter month. Multiply by thirty ranges, and you can see how they add up to several million per season. But it is during the putrid snows of spring that the avalanche reaches its deadliest zenith.

Relatively few occur in ski areas, where avalanche control has become a near science, and well-trained patrols set them off under controlled conditions before they have a chance to "crack." But neither do scientists fully understand the whimsical, lethal snowslide—a constant hazard for deep-powder hounds, cross-country skiers, climbers, and the unruly who ski out of bounds.

Ken and I have known a number of people killed or injured in slides. Some were accidents impossible to foresee. Most happened to skiers taking unwise chances. A few were flukes. Shortly after we arrived, a young Aspen housewife was killed in a minor slide when she choked on her chewing gum. Thereafter I made the children open wide and say, "Aaaahh" before going out the door, and any gum was plucked out and trashed.

As Ken declared disgustedly, "Only you, Martie, suffer angst over million-to-one shots like avalanches. Why don't you worry about something really worthwhile, like myocardial infarctions or the economy?"

He was right, of course. Still, with a gaze that would have paralyzed a cobra, I warned our offspring that if they were ever caught off marked trails or skiing posted "Avalanche Areas—Keep Out!", I would burn all their skis and put them on social probation until they were old enough to vote.

Naturally when they were old enough to vote they delightedly recounted for their flustered parents the times they had skied avalanche terrain, jumped deep couloirs and thumbed their turned-up little noses at death and the racer's edge.

The mother and father are always the last to know.

While snowslides proliferated out-of-doors, the dust kitties under the beds with the dogs gave birth to more dust kitties; the refrigerator leftovers grew diseased; both the lodge and its mistress suffered end-of-season prolapse.

On bleak, dreary May days I dragged myself from room to room, desultorily scrubbing drawers and carpets. Spring cleaning a ski lodge, I found, is as overwhelming as tidying up Blenheim Castle.

On bright, sunny days I tackled the landscaping. Although I am an ardent gardener, this was another awesome undertaking. Plunging into virgin Rocky Mountain soil is only a little less arduous than pounding your way around Cape Hatteras in a canoe. Spading dirt and tossing boulders could only be tackled inches at a time. I had to keep reminding myself that if my seventy-year-old hairdresser could do it, so could I.

Then suddenly, as if someone had blown a whistle and let out the factory, everything exploded in banderoles of riotous color. Spring arrived hand in hand with summer. The unloved dandelion turned broad sweeps of field and meadow into breathtaking carpets of glowing gold. Magnificent lilacs, grown tall as conifers since nurturing from slips by homesick miners' wives in the last century, burst into royal purples, pinky whites, and palest lavenders. Forsythia blazed, flowering crab flamed, delicate Japanese pear smote the senses. June, when she arrived in force, was worth the wait. She marched in with banners unfurled, horns blowing, and all stops out.

I reveled in the beauty and the solitude. Like people in the resort business everywhere, Ken and I were a little weary of all those strangers and their ceaseless questions. If one more person had inquired what time the Maroon Bells rang, I believe we would have broken down like old bastinado victims.

Of course by the end of June we were lonelier than anchorites and dying for our first summer guests to arrive.

But for now the Heatherbed was ours alone. Claytie's studio was done and decorated, and she kissed us goodbye with a fervent promise to "keep in constant touch." Ken muttered ungraciously under his breath, "Don't call us, we'll call you." Between housecleaning and landscaping chores, I dusted off the unopened travel sections of *The New York Times* and settled down to long, slothful reads.

It helped that we had moved all of the children into their very own private guest rooms. This gave their limbs, their psyches, and their elders a good stretch. It may have been hell on the guest rooms, but it was invaluable for the children's and our immortal souls.

Naturally we had extra kids on hand. Word had spread that we had this large family and would scarcely notice one more. On that mistaken theory parents had begun shipping us their young by the score, ostensibly to work or ski, often just to get them out of the house. That year we added two preteen boys who arrived for spring vacation and were still on hand for September school matriculation. Later, kids would break legs and hang around until their casts came off, or they were stranded by divorce or other sudden calamities. One eight-year-old, whose pilot father was killed in the Philippines and whose mother was going to seed in a California commune, came to our summer Ride & Swim Camp for three weeks and stayed for three years.

A fine off-season bonus was having our children and their friends to ourselves. After long, leisurely dinners, we lingered over dessert and sang songs in front of scented piñon fires. We worked on enormous, Byzantine jigsaw puzzles. We played Michigan Rummy amid great shouting, wagers, and table pounding. One evening Mike looked around and said, "I just love this family. It's better than having your own Scout troop."

It goes without saying that Ken and I are crazy about kids, but toward the end I had twenty-three children and a bleak, ravaged expression.

By this time our children considered Aspen's ski slopes their personal property and all of the Rocky Mountains their oyster. Suggestions regarding summer visits back East were met with boos of derision. The kids loved everything about the West and Westerners and had clearly been transplanted for life. As they grew older they too would make midnight rescues and repairs, pound thumbs to pulps, miter a mean sheet, tote hay, lift luggage, wrangle horses and complain about their hard lot in life. But as young adults they agreed, "Thank God you brought us west and trained us for life at hard labor."

They got their start that first spring and summer. We built miles of dry-stone walls, harvested tons of rock from future lawn areas, blasted out a road to the Lower Forty and shooed away a pride of very busy beavers flooding us like the Zuider Zee. In addition, we were soon stocking ponds with trout, building horse corrals and a tack room, planting pasture and constructing pens for Robin's and Mike's 4-H lambs.

Then, of course, there was the summer theater.

On July first we would open, in conjunction with Walt Smith's Hindquarter Restaurant, the first summer stock theater on the western slopes. Old theater friends were already beating their way west as fast as their ancient car would carry them. They would produce, direct, and with their children, reside at—you guessed it—Ye Olde Heath-erbed Inne, Resthouse & Asylum.

Just about the only thing I hadn't planned was a reception for Halley's Comet in 1985.

An era is gone. And with it, Ken's and my youth. We gave it away to hundreds of charming skiers, dozens of wonderful ski bums, and to our beloved children. We never made any money, but we feel blessed to have been part of that warm, zany era of harebrained hoteliers, knight-errant workers, and delightfully ingenuous kids.

Looking back, I sometimes feel nostalgic, sometimes sad, seldom sorry. Most of the time I simply feel twenty years younger.